Teacher's Guide to
Let's Discover the Bible

by
Martin S. Saiewitz

Creation
Adam and Eve ▪ Noah
The Tower of Babel ▪ Abraham and Sarah
Isaac and Rebecca ▪ Jacob and Esau
Joseph and His Brothers ▪ Baby Moses ▪ Let My People Go
Moses on the Mountain ▪ Samson ▪ Ruth and Naomi
David and Goliath ▪ Solomon, the Wise King
Jonah and the Great Fish

©1992 by Behrman House, Inc.
235 Watchung Avenue, West Orange, New Jersey 07052
ISBN 0-8-7441-543-8

CONTENTS

Introduction 3

SET 1

Story 1   Creation 5

Story 2   Adam and Eve 9

Story 3   Noah 13

Story 4   The Tower of Babel 17

Story 5   Abraham and Sarah 21

Story 6   Isaac and Rebecca 25

Story 7   Jacob and Esau 29

Story 8   Joseph and His Brothers 33

SET 2

Story 9   Baby Moses 37

Story 10   Let My People Go 41

Story 11   Moses on the Mountain 45

Story 12   Samson 49

Story 13   Ruth and Naomi 53

Story 14   David and Goliath 57

Story 15   Solomon, The Wise King 61

Story 16   Jonah and the Great Fish 65

WORKSHEETS .... 69 – 95

❑ Introduction

The purpose of the *Teacher's Guide to Let's Discover the Bible* is to provide you with the tools to teach 16 Bible stories the way you want to teach them. The Teacher's Guide will provide you with a variety of activities and teaching suggestions to enhance your students' comprehension and enjoyment of the 16 stories.

This resource should be used as the title suggests—*as a guide.* You are free to try all of the activities, ask all of the questions provided, and utilize all of the worksheets. However, feel free to skip what doesn't seem appropriate for your children. Only you know the level of ability of your students; only you know how you like to teach.

❑ The Teaching Plan

The lesson plan that accompanies each story always begins with **Background for the Teacher** and **Motivation**. The background feature provides you with information related to the story, such as historical references and descriptions of key themes. The motivation activity will help you to introduce the story. The activities are designed to be used either prior to the distribution of the story folder or prior to reading the story.

You will find several features located throughout the lesson plan—**Vocabulary**, **Using the Illustration**, and **Teaching the Story**. The vocabulary feature highlights terms that are often difficult for young readers. The illustration activities will help you make the most use of the colorful illustrations by Lane Yerkes found throughout the story folders. **Teaching the Story** provides you with several suggested questions per page to guide the children through the reading. Occasionally the questions seek responses that tie-in directly to a story's major theme.

Another special feature found at different locations are special "notes." These notes provide either key themes, facts related to the stories, or suggested activities for the classroom.

Hands-On Learning The activities in this feature are designed to bring the story out of the folder and into the children's hands and minds. Several of the **Hands-On Learning** activities are games which can be adapted to your class size.

Another feature that will provide a hands-on learning experience is the **Arts and Crafts** activities which appear in the lesson plans of several stories. Additional craft ideas may be found in *Integrating Arts and Crafts in the Jewish School* by Carol Tauben and Edith Abrams, which is available from Behrman House.

Another feature which utilizes other sources is **Read More About It**, which references stories in *Exploring Our Living Past* by Laura Simms, et. al., *Stories from Our Living Past* by Francine Prose, and *Lessons from Our Living Past* by Seymour Rossel, et. al. All three titles are available from Behrman House.

Activity Page Each of the story folders ends with an activity page. Solutions for the activities and suggestions for non-readers are provided in the lesson plan.

Let's Talk About It This feature provides a theme-based discussion question which you can use to explore your students' understanding of a main theme for each story. You should use the question to promote independent, critical thinking.

Family Education Learning at Home worksheets are provided in the back of this text. They can be duplicated and distributed to be taken home by the children. These worksheets provide an opportunity for enriching the study of Judaism in the home.

For some stories, **Class Enrichment** replaces Learning at Home. This feature provides optional classroom experiences. These worksheets also appear in the back of this text. All worksheets are numbered to match the story number.

CREATION

In the beginning, God made heaven and earth. God said, "Let there be light." And there was light. God saw that the light was good, and God separated light from darkness. God called the light Day, and the darkness Night. Then there was evening and there was morning—the first day.

God said, "Let there be space to separate the water above from the water below." And so it was. God called the space Sky. Then there was evening and there was morning—the second day.

❑ Motivation

Provide each child with a piece of paper and a pencil or crayon. Tell them to draw "something" using only circles and offer no further directions. The children will probably draw a variety of objects. Give another piece of paper to each child and then show them how to create a flower using only circles. After they have drawn one ask: Would you have made a flower without the directions? (perhaps, but only by chance) Explain that something made with a purpose has directions or plans. Just as they needed directions to make the flower, a builder needs architect's plans to build a house. In this way, when God created the universe, God worked from a plan.

❑ Biblical Source

Genesis 1:1–2:4

❑ Background for the Teacher

Many ancient civilizations had a story of creation. Among the elements that distinguish our Judaic version from others is the concept of a purposeful plan. Many mythological versions of creation focus on power struggles between gods. The result of such a struggle is the creation of the world. Another version of creation is the idea of a mother god giving birth to the heavens, earth, water, fire, and so on. The story of creation presented here is a story of one God creating according to Divine plan—not by accident or coincidence. This is the major import of the story to be taught to the children.

❑ Vocabulary

creation the bringing of the world into existence out of nothing

❑ Using the Illustration

After reading the first page, ask the children to describe what the illustration represents. *(creation of heaven and earth, day and night, sky)*

❑ Teaching the Story

Q: What did God make first?
God made heaven and earth.

Q: What else did God make on the first day?
Light and day and night were made on the first day.

Q: Why would God choose to make light on the first day?
Answers may vary. God created light before creating the world to see the work.

CREATION **5**

❑ Teaching the Story

Q: What did God call the dry land and the deep waters?
God called them earth and seas.

Q: What living things were created on the fifth day?
God filled the waters and the sky—sea creatures, the lizards, and birds of every kind.

> *The light created by God on the first day didn't shine from the sun—it came directly from God.*

God said, "Let the dry land appear." And so it was. God called the dry land Earth, and the deep waters God called Seas. Then God said, "Let plants grow, and fruit trees, too." And so it was. And God saw that it was good. Then there was evening and there was morning—the third day.

God said, "Let there be lights in the sky to mark the days and the years—and to shine upon the earth." And so it was. God made the sun to shine by day, and the moon and stars to shine by night. And God saw that this was good. Then there was evening and there was morning—the fourth day.

God said, "Let the waters fill with living things, and let there be birds to fly in the sky above the earth." So God created the great sea creatures, the lizards, and birds of every kind. And God saw that this was good. God blessed the living things, saying, "Have many babies and fill the skies and seas." And there was evening and there was morning—the fifth day.

God said, "Let there be living things on the earth—cattle, insects, and wild beasts of every kind." And so it was. And God saw that it was good. And God said, "Let us make human beings that are like us." And God created people—men and

Hands-on Learning

Creation Identification Game To play this game you will need a die and seven pieces of construction paper. Write the numbers one to seven on the construction paper; one numeral on each piece of paper. Tape the seven numerals around your classroom.

Each child takes a turn rolling the die. Whichever number appears on the die, the child should run to that number on the wall and identify something created on that numbered day of creation. If they answer correctly, they should run to the number seven to "rest."

6 LET'S DISCOVER THE BIBLE

women, God created them. Then God blessed them and said, "Have many babies and fill the earth. You must care for the fish of the sea, the birds of the sky, and all the things that live on the earth."

God told the people, "Behold, I give you the plants and the trees—eat the fruit. And I give the green plants to all the animals of the land and the birds of the sky for food." And it was so. And God looked at all that God had made, and found it very good. Then there was evening and there was morning—the sixth day.

The heaven and the earth—and everything in them—were complete.

On the seventh day God finished working and rested. God called the seventh day *Shabbat*. And God blessed the seventh day and called it holy, because on that day God rested from the work of creation.

And that is the story of how the heaven and the earth were created.

❑ Teaching the Story

Q: **What did God say the people must care for?**
People must care for the fish of the sea, the birds of the sky, and all the things that live on the earth.

Q: **What did God give the people to eat?**
They were given the fruit of the plants and trees.

Q: **Why were people—men and women—created last?**
Discuss the explanation that people would need everything present to survive. The analogy can be drawn that God was as a host who set a table with every delicacy and then welcomed the guests to their places.

Q: **On the seventh day, God finished working and rested. What did God call this day of rest?**
Shabbat is the day of rest.

❑ Vocabulary

behold look upon

At first allow the children to repeat answers already given; the repetition will help them remember. Later, give hints for other possible answers or encourage original responses (for example, "dove" instead of "bird"; "tuna" instead of "fish"). You can set a time limit to end the game or the game can end after everyone has had a turn in the "day of rest."

CREATION

Activity Page

Shadow Match
This exercise is good for developing perception skills as well as for reviewing what was created by God.

Word Find
Possible answers include *car, on, cat, tar, tear,* and *care.* You can also play this game with other words from the lesson, such as SHABBAT (sat, bat, hat, and so on).

You can make the activity more directed by asking for specific words. For example: Which animals can you find in CREATION? (cat, rat) Can you find something to drink in CREATION? (tea) Can you find a word that means the opposite of far? (near) Can you find something to ride in? (car)

Flower Pot
At this time you may want to plant a seed or bring in a potted plant for the children to care for to reinforce the theme of creation throughout the year.

A Big Question
This question should be used as a trigger for classroom discussion. (God created people to take care of the world.)

Let's Talk About It
How is God's creation still continuing all around us?

Answers will vary. With the birth of every person, every animal, and every new plant God continues to create. We are a part of God's creation. People help this ongoing creation by planting flowers, caring for animals, conserving natural resources, and so on.

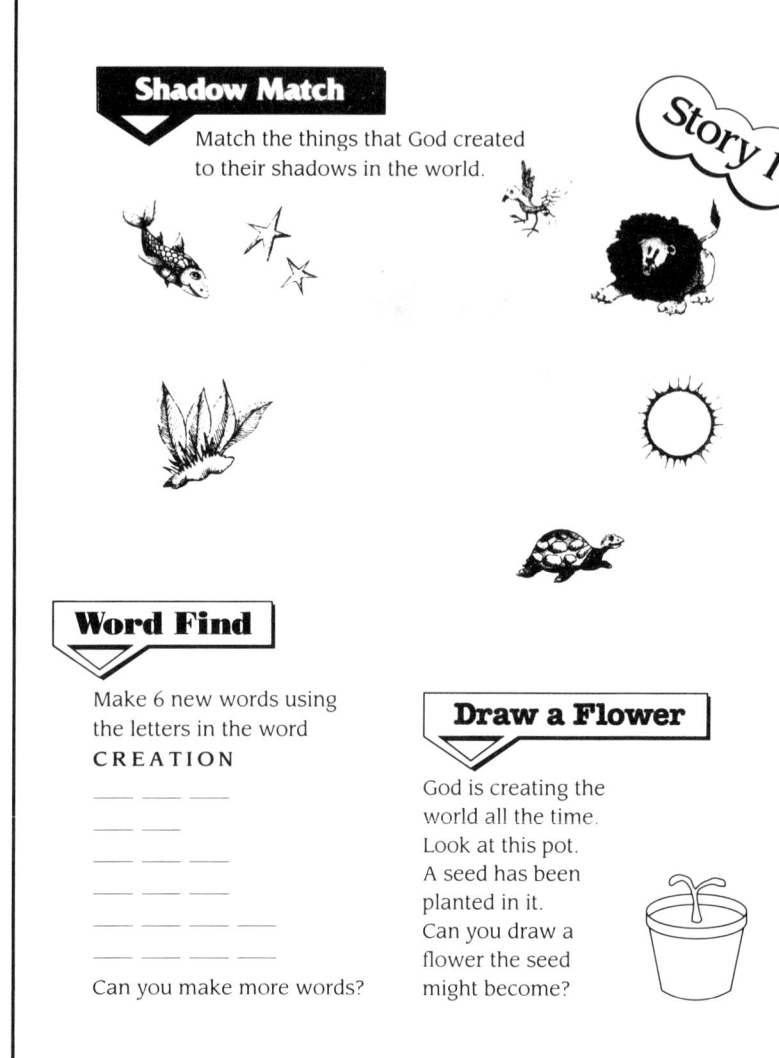

Story 1

Shadow Match
Match the things that God created to their shadows in the world.

Word Find
Make 6 new words using the letters in the word **CREATION**

___ ___
___ ___
___ ___
___ ___
___ ___ ___
___ ___ ___

Can you make more words?

Draw a Flower
God is creating the world all the time. Look at this pot. A seed has been planted in it. Can you draw a flower the seed might become?

Family Education

Learning at Home Duplicate worksheet 1 and distribute copies at the end of class. Have the children bring home both the worksheet and the four-page folder containing the story of *Creation*.

Learning at Home worksheets have been prepared for some of the stories. They provide an opportunity for enriching the study of Judaism in the home. The activities found in the worksheets allow each child's family to participate in the child's education.

Learning at Home Worksheet available on page 71 in the back of this guide.

8 LET'S DISCOVER THE BIBLE

Adam and Eve

God planted a garden in Eden and put Adam, the first man, in the garden. And God said, "You may eat the fruit of every tree, but do not eat the fruit of the tree in the center of the garden. If you eat the fruit of the tree called the tree of knowing good and evil, you will surely die!"

Then God said, "Adam should not be alone. I will create a partner for him." God paraded all the living things in front of Adam and Adam named each one of them—lion, tiger, elephant, goat, zebra, eagle, and dove. But no partner for Adam was found. So God made Adam sleep a deep sleep, and while he slept, God took one of Adam's ribs and from it made a woman named Eve. And when Adam saw Eve, he loved her and they were partners.

❏ Motivation

Have volunteers talk about a time when they did something wrong. How did they feel about what they had done? What happened because of what they did? Were they punished? Ask them to consider what they learned from the experience. Perhaps you can relate an appropriate experience from your own childhood.

❏ Using the Illustration

After reading the first page, ask the children questions about the illustration, such as: Who is the man in the picture? Where is he? What is he doing? Can you name the animals in the picture? Can you name other animals?

❏ Biblical Source

Genesis 2:5–24

❏ Background for the Teacher

The story of Adam and Eve is an allegory which should not be taken literally. It is not so much the story of a talking snake as it is a story of the struggle between the good and evil in all of us. Every person makes moral choices. Each of us must choose between what is right and what is wrong. An important focus for your pupils is the effects or consequences of these choices.

The story of Adam and Eve can be viewed as a second story of creation. God creates the Garden of Eden and places Adam, the first man, in it with all of the living things created by God. Then God creates Eve as a partner for Adam. An important theme to develop is that God created Eve because people need each other for companionship and support.

❏ Teaching the Story

Q: **Who was the first man?**
Adam was the first man.

Q: **From what tree could Adam not eat the fruit?**
Adam could not eat from the tree of knowing good and evil.

Q: **What did God say would happen to Adam if he ate the fruit?**
Adam would die.

Q: **What was Eve made from?**
Eve was made from one of Adam's ribs.

❑ Teaching the Story

Q: What was the sliest creature God made?
The snake was the sliest creature.

Q: What did the snake say to Eve?
The snake told Eve that she could eat the fruit and not die.

Q: What happened when Adam and Eve ate the fruit?
They knew things they had not known before.

Q: Why did Adam and Eve hide when they heard God's voice?
Perhaps they knew they had done something wrong.

❑ Vocabulary

sliest   most skillful at clever tricks
delicious   very pleasing to the taste
forbidden   not to be used

It is not written in the Bible that the forbidden fruit was an apple.

NOW in the garden was a snake. The snake was the sliest creature God had made. The snake spoke to Eve, saying, "Go ahead, eat the fruit of the tree in the middle of the garden. I promise, you will not die. But God knows that as soon as you eat that fruit, your eyes will be opened."

Eve looked at the tree and its fruit looked more delicious than the fruit of any other tree in the garden. So Eve ate the fruit of that tree, and she gave some to Adam and he ate, also. Suddenly, they knew things they had not known before. They saw that they were naked, and they sewed fig leaves together to make clothing.

When they heard God's voice, they hid among the trees. But God found them and said, "Who told you that you were naked? Did you eat the fruit of the forbidden tree?" And Adam and Eve told God about the snake and all that had happened.

❑ Ask and Answer

Have each child prepare a question to ask either Adam, Eve, or the snake. Let the children role-play by answering the questions. You may want to divide the class into groups of Adams, Eves, and snakes.

Examples:
   Adam, why did you eat the fruit?
   Eve, why did you listen to the snake?
   Snake, why did you trick Eve?
   Adam, how did you feel when you heard God's voice calling you?

LET'S DISCOVER THE BIBLE

God spoke to the snake. "Because you have done this," God said, "you shall be the lowest of the animals. You shall crawl on your belly and eat dirt all the days of your life. And all women will hate you."

To Eve, God said, "You will suffer, too, for listening to the snake. You will have children, but it will be painful for you."

And to Adam, God said, "Since you also disobeyed me, you must be punished too. You shall have to work hard from morning to night to force the earth to give you food. You came from the earth and, on the day you die, you will return to the earth."

Then God made clothing from animal skins for Adam and Eve, and dressed them. And God sent Adam and Eve out of the Garden of Eden, so that they might never eat the fruit of the other forbidden tree—the tree of life that lasts forever.

❑ Vocabulary

disobeyed did not follow directions or orders

❑ Teaching the Story

Q: How was the snake punished?
Snakes were made the lowest of the animals.

Q: Why were Adam and Eve sent from the Garden of Eden?
Adam and Eve were sent from the Garden of Eden for disobeying God and so that they would not eat the fruit of the other forbidden tree—the tree of life that lasts forever.

Read More About It

"Adam and Eve and the Very First Darkness," Exploring Our Living Past, p. 118. The story, taken from the Midrash, describes Adam and Eve's first encounter with night.

"The First Farmer," Stories from Our Living Past, p. 96. The Garden of Eden was a place of wonder and delight. Yet the Bible tells us that God put Adam there "to till and look after it."

Hands-on Learning

Divide the class into groups and provide each group with colored clay. Have them make characters from the story—the snake, Adam, Eve, and the Tree of Knowledge. As they make their figures, discuss the features of the story with the children in each group. After they have finished, discuss how their creation is like God's creation of the world. Compare how they may have made Adam from clay and that the Torah describes Adam being made from dust. Relate the Hebrew word *adama* (earth) to the name Adam. You can create a classroom diorama to house the clay figures.

Activity Page

Scrambled Animals

For Readers: How many other animals can they think of? Write them on the chalkboard as they are named.

For Non-Readers: Turn the scrambled letters into riddles for the children. Example: I am thinking of an animal in the Garden of Eden that begins with the sound "L" and roars.

Missing Letters

For Readers: Ask volunteers to read the completed sentences aloud to the class.

For Non-Readers: Read each sentence aloud to the children, leaving one word out. Ask the children to supply the missing word.

Find the Twins

This exercise is appropriate for readers and non-readers to develop perception skills.

A Big Question

Each activity page in the program ends with **A Big Question**. Each of these questions highlights a key concept in the Bible story and should be used as a trigger for an open-ended class discussion. You might like to record and keep the interesting responses. When given the opportunity, children will often surprise us with their insights and comments.

Let's Talk About It

Why did God create a partner for Adam? Answers will vary. God decided that Adam should not be alone. Expand the discussion by asking the children why God would not want Adam to be alone. Ask: Why do we need other people?

❑ Classrooom Enrichment (Optional)

Worksheets for classroom enrichment are provided for some of the stories. Duplicate and distribute worksheet 2. The children can complete and color the picture as an activity during class or at home.

Enrichment worksheet available on page 73 in the back of this guide.

12 LET'S DISCOVER THE BIBLE

NOAH

In the days when people did evil on the earth, there was one good man who became God's favorite. His name was Noah.

God spoke to Noah. "Soon I will destroy all living things on the earth in a great flood, but you will be my partner in making a new world." God said, "Make an ark—a huge wooden boat. Bring into the ark two of every living thing—male and female, to stay alive." And Noah started building an ark as God commanded.

One day, God said to Noah, "In seven days' time, I will make rain to fall. It will rain for forty days and forty nights, and all that breathes on earth will die. Go into the ark, you and all your family. And take all the animals, as I told you, to keep them alive with you." And Noah did all that God commanded.

❏ Using the Illustration

Have the children think about the purpose of the ark as they examine the illustration.

Why is the ark so large?
The ark had to be large to have room for all the animals.

Why are there no windows?
Noah did not want water to come into the ark.

How could Noah steer the ark?
Noah couldn't steer the ark—it was just meant to float until the flood stopped.

❏ Biblical Source

Genesis 6:5–9:17

❏ Background for the Teacher

Floods are common in the Tigris-Euphrates river valley. This region, also known as Mesopotamia, was home to a succession of civilizations. The biblical account of Noah and the Great Flood bears a striking similarity to flood stories of Mesopotamian origin. Because floods are not common in Palestine and the Mesopotamian accounts predate the Hebrew text, scholars believe that the Israelites borrowed the story and adapted it to fit their beliefs.

❏ Motivation

Talk about rainbows with the children. Ask questions such as, Who has seen a rainbow? What colors did you see? When did you see the rainbow? Tell the children that rainbows have a special meaning which they will learn about in the story of Noah.

❏ Teaching the Story

Q: Why was Noah God's favorite?
In the time when people did evil on the earth, Noah was the one good man.

Q: Why would God want to destroy all living things?
They did evil.

Q: What is an ark?
An ark is a huge wooden boat.

Q: Who was on the ark with Noah?
Noah brought his family and two of every living thing on the ark.

❏ Teaching the Story

Q: For how long did it rain?
It rained for forty days and forty nights.

Q: After the waters began to go down, where did the ark come to rest?
The ark came to rest on top of Mt. Ararat.

Q: Why did Noah send out a raven and a dove?
They were sent to find out if it was safe to leave the ark. If they didn't come back, Noah would know that they had found a dry place on which to land.

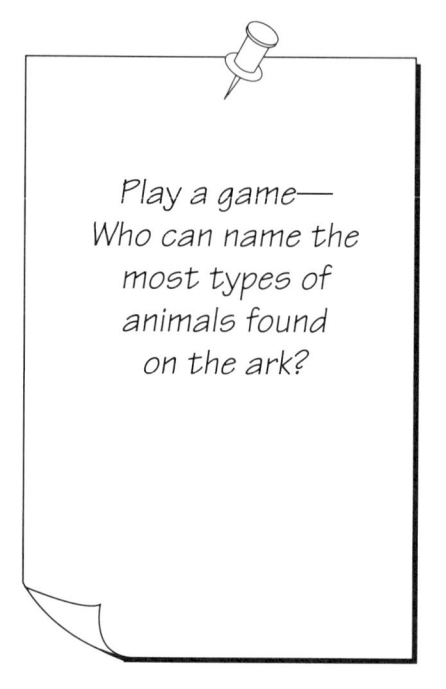

Play a game—Who can name the most types of animals found on the ark?

Seven days later, the fountains of the deep burst and the windows of the skies opened and rain fell. For forty days and forty nights the rain poured down on the earth. The flood of waters covered all the land—from the smallest hill to the highest mountain. Every living thing on earth was drowned. But Noah and his wife and children, and all the animals with them in the ark, rode safely upon the waves on top of the waters.

The waters covered the earth one hundred and fifty days, and then God remembered Noah and the ark. God made a wind to blow across the earth and the waters began to go down. The fountains of the deep were stopped up, the windows of heaven closed, and the rain stopped falling from the skies. Another one hundred and fifty days passed before the ark came to rest on top of a mountain called Ararat.

Finally Noah opened the window of the ark. He sent out a black bird, the raven. But the raven could find no place to rest, for the trees were still covered with water. Then Noah sent out a dove. But the dove could find no place to rest, and it returned to the ark. Noah waited seven days more, and sent the dove out again. As night was falling, the dove returned. In its beak, it carried a small branch of an olive tree. Seven more days passed, and Noah sent the dove out once again. This time it did not return, so Noah knew that it was safe to leave the ark.

Hands-on Learning

Have the children draw animal faces on oaktag paper and make masks from the drawings. A string or a rubberband can be used to hold the mask in place. Have the children tell the story of Noah and the ark from their perspective as animals on the ark. (Example: "I'm a rabbit. Noah caught me and my partner in the forest and brought us on to the ark. I got seasick. He kept the wolves away from us because we don't get along. I was glad when we got off the ark.")

14 LET'S DISCOVER THE BIBLE

God spoke to Noah, saying, "Come out of the ark. Bring your family and all the living things with you."

Then Noah opened the door of the ark, and all the creatures came out: elephants and geese, camels and goats, mice and giraffes, turtles and wolves—together with all the young ones they had while on the ark."

And Noah put stones together as an altar to God and thanked God with a burning sacrifice. And God smelled the pleasant odor of Noah's sacrifice and said, "I will not destroy the world again. From now on, summer and winter, day and night shall never end. Whenever it rains and you see a rainbow, it will be a sign."

And so God promised never again to destroy the earth with a flood, and gave us the rainbow as a reminder.

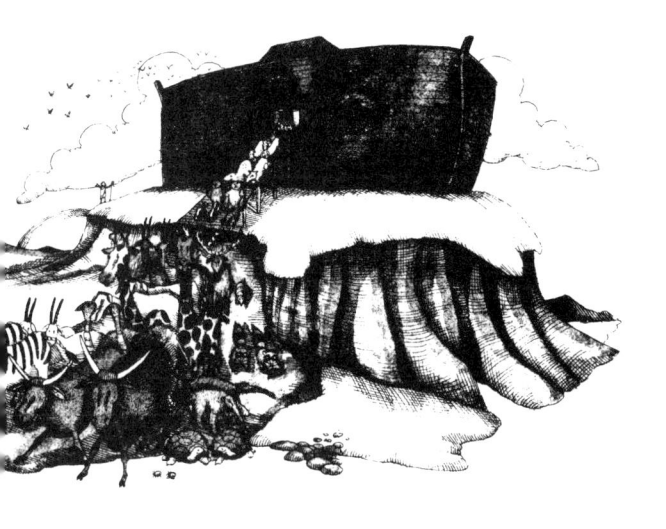

❏ Teaching the Story

Q: How did Noah thank God?
He thanked God with a burning sacrifice.

Q: How do we know that God will never again destroy the earth?
The rainbow is a sign—a reminder—that God will not destroy the earth.

❏ Vocabulary

altar a raised place used for worship or sacrifice

sacrifice an act of offering something precious to God

Read More About It

"The Great Flood," <u>Exploring Our Living Past</u>, p. 127. This longer version of the story of Noah and the Great Flood explores the moral that God rewards goodness and punishes evil.

"The Lie Takes a Partner," <u>Stories from Our Living Past</u>, p. 20. This clever story explains how evil and dishonesty could continue after the Great Flood.

Activity Page

Noah's Animal Puzzle
After the children have completed the exercise independently, discuss some of the differences between grown-up and baby animal names. Examples include: cat/kitten, dog/puppy, bear/cub, cow/calf, duck/duckling, deer/fawn.

Color By Letter
This experience is suitable for readers and non-readers, but you may have to assist children who can not yet read with the letter/color code in the center of the rainbow.

A Big Question
The sight of a rainbow in the sky has always held a great fascination for children and for adults as well. Use the question as a trigger for an open-ended class discussion. Encourage the children to explain if and how the Noah story has changed the way they think about rainbows. You might want to record and keep the interesting responses. When given the opportunity, children often surprise us with their insights and comments.

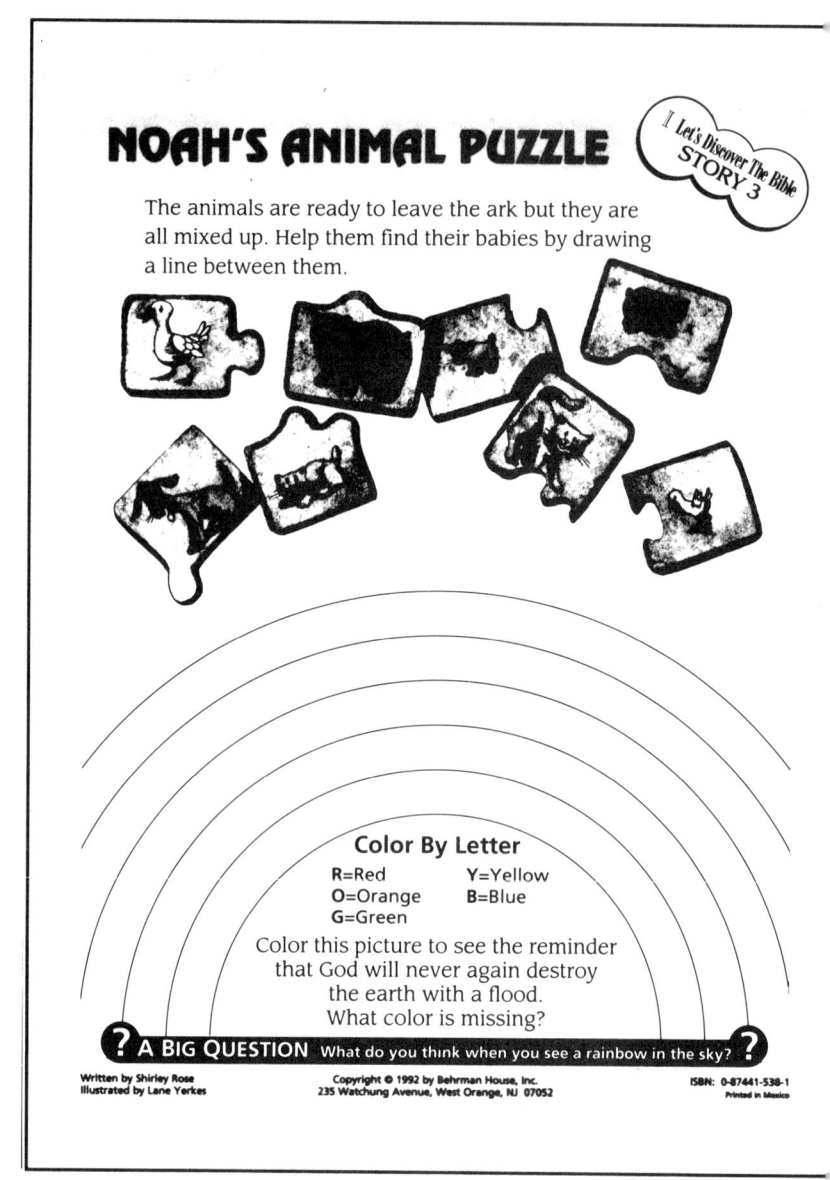

Let's Talk About It
Do you think people in the world can become so wicked that God would bring another Great Flood?
Answers will vary. God will not because God promised not to destroy the earth with a flood. The rainbow serves as a reminder of this promise.

NOAH'S ANIMAL PUZZLE
Let's Discover The Bible STORY 3

The animals are ready to leave the ark but they are all mixed up. Help them find their babies by drawing a line between them.

Color By Letter
R=Red Y=Yellow
O=Orange B=Blue
G=Green

Color this picture to see the reminder that God will never again destroy the earth with a flood.
What color is missing?

A BIG QUESTION What do you think when you see a rainbow in the sky?

Written by Shirley Rose
Illustrated by Lane Yerkes
Copyright © 1992 by Behrman House, Inc.
235 Watchung Avenue, West Orange, NJ 07052
ISBN: 0-87441-538-1
Printed in Mexico

❏ Classroom Enrichment (Optional)
Make a model of the ark using a brown shopping bag, a small box, stapler and scissors. Cut two wide strips of paper from the bag. Place them on either side of the box and staple them at opposite ends to form the bow and stern of the ark. Ask the children to bring in pictures of animals. They can draw the pictures at home or cut them from magazines. (Be sure to tell them to get permission before cutting!) Decorate the ark with the pictures.

The Tower of Babel

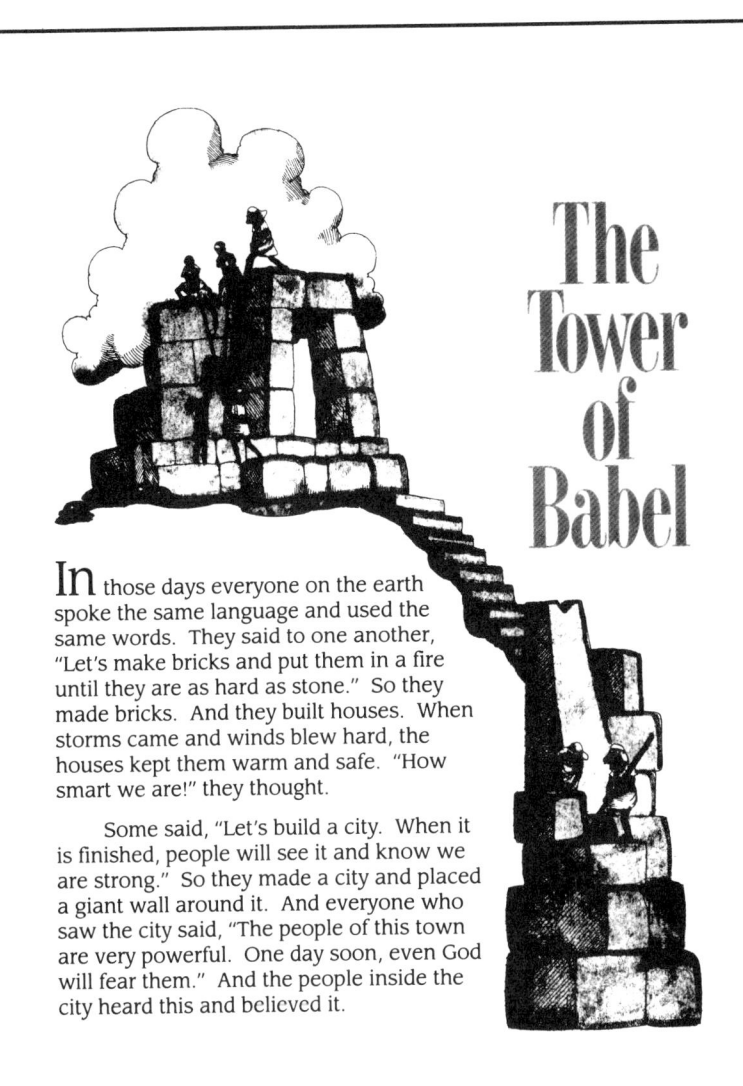

In those days everyone on the earth spoke the same language and used the same words. They said to one another, "Let's make bricks and put them in a fire until they are as hard as stone." So they made bricks. And they built houses. When storms came and winds blew hard, the houses kept them warm and safe. "How smart we are!" they thought.

Some said, "Let's build a city. When it is finished, people will see it and know we are strong." So they made a city and placed a giant wall around it. And everyone who saw the city said, "The people of this town are very powerful. One day soon, even God will fear them." And the people inside the city heard this and believed it.

❏ Motivation

Tell the class that there was a time when people spoke the same language. Today there are many different languages. Ask them to think of reasons why this change occurred. (Answers will vary.) Ask them to name as many different languages as they can.

❏ Biblical Source

Genesis 11:1–9

❏ Background for the Teacher

Like the story of Noah, the Tower of Babel may have Mesopotamian origins. Pyramid-shaped temples called ziggurats which were built in this region may have been the inspiration for this story. Also the description of baking bricks matches the early development of brickmaking in the ancient world.

There is a child-like quality to the people in this story. Children like to build tall towers with their blocks. The critical theme in this story is that the people of the city wished to replace God. They felt that their work was greater than God's. Point this out to the children by showing how the people bragged about their greatness and how they declared their desire to be seen as gods. This theme is emphasized in the questions for this story.

❏ Teaching the Story

Q: Why does the story begin with "In those days everyone spoke the same language"?
Many languages are spoken today.

Q: Why did the people brag about their bricks?
They thought they were very smart for making the bricks.

Q: What did the people hear that they believed?
They believed that they were powerful and one day even God would fear them.

❑ Teaching the Story

Q: Why were the people of the city behaving badly?
They became conceited about the work they had done.

Q: How did God punish the people?
He made them speak different languages so that they couldn't talk to each other.

Q: What happened to the tower?
The people stopped building the tower.

Q: Why did the people scatter all over the world?
They went looking for others who spoke the same language.

❑ Vocabulary

mighty powerful
admire to look at with a feeling of approval
marvelous of the highest quality
jealous resentful feelings toward a rival
jumbled mixed in a confused way
babbling meaningless sounds
scattered separated in different directions

They said, "Come let us build a mighty tower high up into the sky. When it is done, we will live in heaven, and people will call us gods." And they began building the tower. Brick by brick, level by level, they made it higher and higher. Every day they stopped to admire their work, saying, "Even God has never built anything so marvelous." And every night they looked up at the tower and said, "Look at what we have created! How wonderful we are!"

God looked down at the city and the tower. "People should not behave like this," God thought. "They have one language: they could be friends and learn more about each other. They have one language: they could make peace with everyone on earth. But these people want to make other people jealous and to rule over them."

And so God decided to punish these people to teach them a lesson.

The next morning, as they did every day, the people went back to work on the tower. But, now, when the leaders said, "Bring up another brick," the workers did not understand them. And when the workers said, "We are thirsty and we need water," the leaders did not understand them. In fact, even the workers did not understand one another! They used the same words as always, but the words came out in many languages.

From the bottom of the tower to the top, everyone talked and talked, but no one understood a word that was spoken. Jumbled all together, they sounded like babbling—the babbling of a brook.

In the end the people gave up trying to build the tower and they left the city. They scattered all over the earth, making new friends, looking for other people who spoke the same language they did. Everywhere they went they told their story.

And that is how God stopped the building of the mighty tower and turned it into a "Tower of Babel."

Hands-on Learning

Bring to class a set of building blocks (cardboard or wood). Perhaps you can borrow them from a nursery school. Tell the children to build a tower of blocks in the middle of the room. Then have the class try to build the tower again but to talk only gibberish. When they finish, ask them to describe the difficulties they encountered when they couldn't communicate with one another.

LET'S DISCOVER THE BIBLE

❑ Using the Illustration

Tell the class that the picture on this page is how one artist thinks the Tower of Babel looked. Ask the children how their image of the tower differed from the one shown here. You may ask the children to draw their idea of how the tower looked. Display the pictures and ask volunteers to explain their drawings.

> *By the end of the story, the children should recognize the pun between the words Babel and babble.*

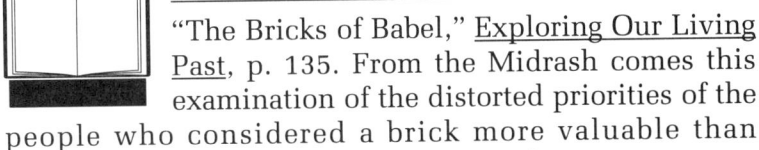

Read More About It

"The Bricks of Babel," <u>Exploring Our Living Past</u>, p. 135. From the Midrash comes this examination of the distorted priorities of the people who considered a brick more valuable than human life. An abbreviated version of this story appears on **Learning at Home**, worksheet #4 in this guide.

Activity Page

Tower Maze
Children always enjoy mazes and readers and non-readers alike will be able to complete this activity. You can too, of course, but to save you the time and trouble, path #3 is the one that goes to the top of the tower.

Word Find
For Readers: The people could have been FRIENDS
For Non-Readers: Find and circle the words. Say a sentence with each word.

More Things To Do
1. *Examples:* power, sour, hour, shower.
2. *For Non-Readers:* Ask the children to think of words that begin with the B sound.
3. *For Non-Readers:* Ask the children to think of words that begin with the sounds R, O, and T.

A Big Question
A class discussion focusing on this question will undoubtedly help to clarify the youngsters' values about what things are really important. The children's answers to the question should prove to be very interesting. Be sure to record some of them.

Let's Talk About It
How does the story of the Tower of Babel show God's desire to make each person special?
Answers will vary but may focus on the idea that by creating different languages for people God makes each person unique.

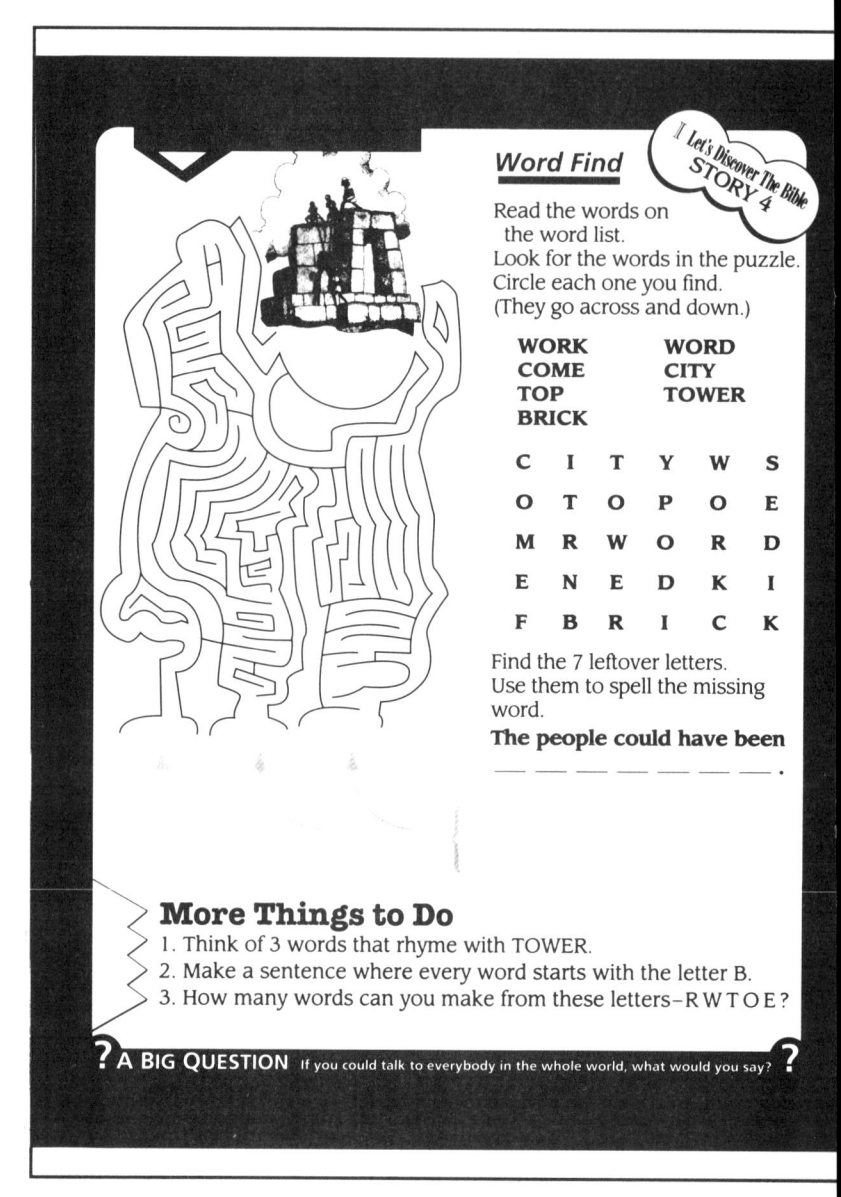

Let's Discover The Bible STORY 4

Word Find
Read the words on the word list.
Look for the words in the puzzle.
Circle each one you find.
(They go across and down.)

WORK	WORD
COME	CITY
TOP	TOWER
BRICK	

C	I	T	Y	W	S
O	T	O	P	O	E
M	R	W	O	R	D
E	N	E	D	K	I
F	B	R	I	C	K

Find the 7 leftover letters. Use them to spell the missing word.

The people could have been _ _ _ _ _ _ _ .

More Things to Do
1. Think of 3 words that rhyme with TOWER.
2. Make a sentence where every word starts with the letter B.
3. How many words can you make from these letters–R W T O E?

? A BIG QUESTION If you could talk to everybody in the whole world, what would you say? **?**

Family Education
Learning at Home The *Learning at Home* worksheets provide an opportunity for enriching the study of Judaism in the home. The activities found in the worksheets allow each child's family to participate in the child's education.

Distribute worksheet 4 at the end of class. Have the children bring home both the worksheet and the four-page folder containing the story of *The Tower of Babel*.

Learning at Home worksheet available on page 75 in the back of this guide.

Abraham and Sarah

God said to Abraham: "Leave your father's house. Go to the land I will show you. I will bless you and make you into a great nation." And Abraham did as God commanded.

Abraham and Sarah, his wife, crossed the river and started out for the Land of Canaan. Abraham's nephew, Lot, went with them. They took their sheep and their cattle and all that they had.

When they arrived in Canaan, God said to Abraham, "This is the land I promised to you. Your people will live in this land forever." And Abraham set up his tent and thanked God.

The sheep and the cattle gave birth to lambs and calves, and the herds grew. Soon it was hard to tell which animals belonged to Abraham and which belonged to Lot. The shepherds began to quarrel with one another.

❏ Motivation

By offering to divide the land with Lot, even giving him the choice of the better land, Abraham establishes the idea of peace in a family. Shalom Bayit—peace at home—is an idea that children can understand in the context of fairness and sharing to keep peace.

Bring cookies (or something similar) to class that can be divided up or shared. Ask the class to decide how to share the item. Try to make the item something that is not easy to divide equally. Tie-in the discussion of how to divide the cookies to the idea of fairness to keep harmony and peace among friends.

❏ Biblical Source

Genesis 11:26–19:29

❏ Background for the Teacher

The story of Abraham and Sarah is filled with different themes that can be focused upon with your class. These themes include devotion to God, as shown by Abraham; the covenant between God and the people Israel; the principle of Shalom Bayit, peace at home; and, the belief that God does not harm the good when punishing the evil. You should consider which of these themes you wish to cover based on the constraints of your class time and the children's abilities. The questions listed under Teaching the Story will help you develop these themes.

❏ Teaching the Story

God told Abraham to leave his father's house and go to a land that God would show to Abraham.

Q: What did Abraham do?
Abraham did as God commanded.

Q: Who went with Abraham to Canaan?
Sarah and Lot went with Abraham.

Q: How does Abraham feel about God?
Answers will vary. You may want to draw responses that focus on Abraham's devotion to God.

❏ Vocabulary

bless to make holy
nation a community of people
shepherd a person who takes care of sheep
quarrel argue

❑ Teaching the Story

Q: Why did the shepherds begin to quarrel?
It was hard to tell which animals belonged to Lot and which ones belonged to Abraham.

Q: How did Abraham solve the problem?
He offered to divide the land between himself and Lot.

Q: Lot took the better land for his herds. Was this fair to Abraham?
Probably not, but Abraham was willing to give more, and take less, to keep peace and friendship with Lot.

Q: Why did Abraham and Sarah name their child Isaac?
Isaac means "Child of Laughter"—Sarah laughed when God told her she would have a child.

❑ Creating a Directory of Names

Write the name Isaac on a piece of construction paper (in both English and Hebrew if appropriate for your class). Next to the name(s) draw a large smiling face. Have each child write their English (and Hebrew) name(s) on a piece of construction paper. Ask the children to draw something that they associate with their names. Do the children know for whom they were named?

While there are no Jewish laws regarding the naming of children, Eastern European custom dictates that the child be named in the memory of a family ancestor. (Sephardim often name children for living relatives.)

Abraham said to his nephew Lot, "Let there be peace between us, and among our shepherds. Choose whatever part of the land you want, and I will take the rest." Lot took the green, grassy land near the city of Sodom, beside the Jordan River. He left the brown, stony hills of Canaan for Abraham. They hugged and went their separate ways.

God spoke again to Abraham. "Sarah will soon have your child," God said. Now Sarah was in the door of her tent, listening, and she began to laugh. "Why do you laugh?" God asked.

"You know I am too old to have a child," Sarah said. But God answered, "Have faith. Nothing is too difficult for God!" And it was so. In nine months time, Sarah gave birth to a baby boy. Abraham and Sarah called the boy, Isaac, which means "child of laughter."

God said to Abraham, "People in the valley near the Jordan River are very evil. I will destroy the cities of Sodom and Gomorrah."

But Abraham spoke up, saying, "You are the God of Justice. Will you destroy good people along with the evil people?"

God said, "If I find fifty innocent people, I will not destroy the cities."

Then Abraham said, "Forgive me for speaking my heart, but what if You find thirty innocent people? Won't You save the cities for the sake of thirty good people?" And God agreed.

Then Abraham said, "Dear God, what if there are only ten innocent people? Won't You save the cities if there are ten good people?"

Hands-on Learning

The children can make a class mural of Abraham and Lot agreeing to go their separate ways. Divide the class into four groups. Spread out a large piece of butcher paper on the floor. On the right side of the paper, have one group draw the grassy land near the city of Sodom. On the left side have another group draw the brown stony hills of Canaan. A third group should draw Abraham and Lot in the middle. The fourth group can draw the shepherds and their herds.

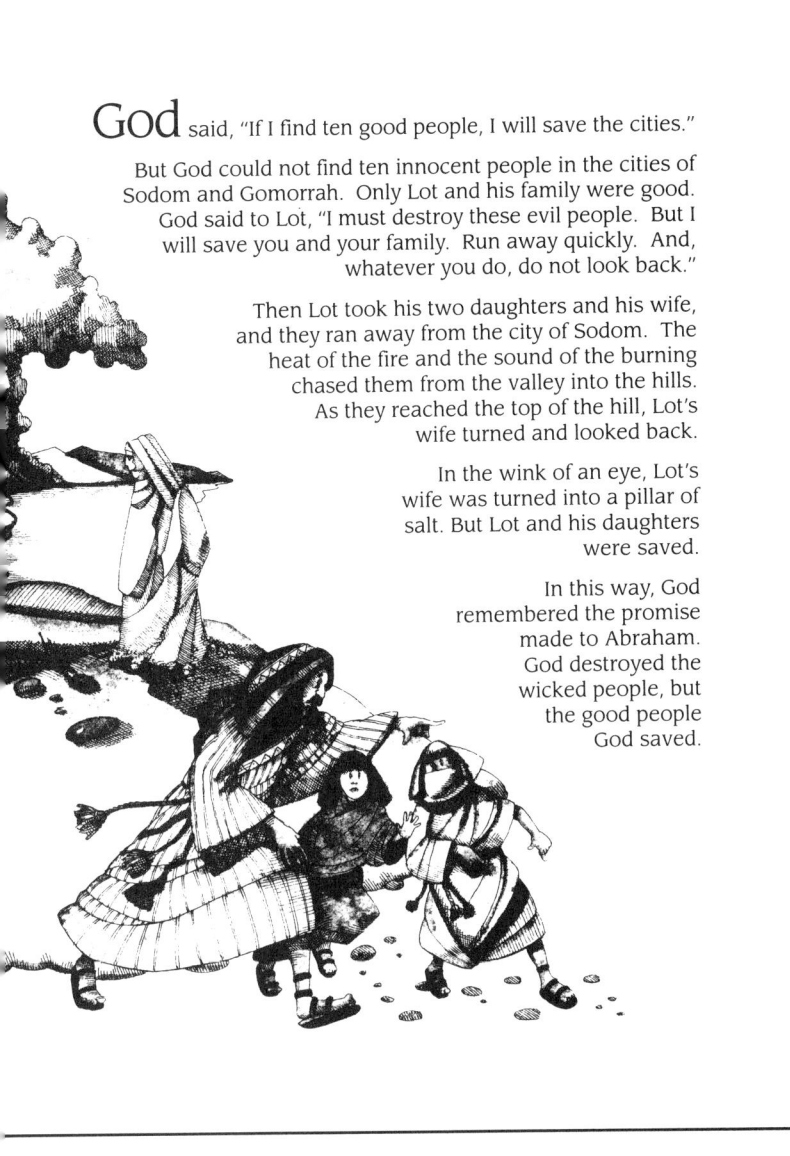

God said, "If I find ten good people, I will save the cities."

But God could not find ten innocent people in the cities of Sodom and Gomorrah. Only Lot and his family were good. God said to Lot, "I must destroy these evil people. But I will save you and your family. Run away quickly. And, whatever you do, do not look back."

Then Lot took his two daughters and his wife, and they ran away from the city of Sodom. The heat of the fire and the sound of the burning chased them from the valley into the hills. As they reached the top of the hill, Lot's wife turned and looked back.

In the wink of an eye, Lot's wife was turned into a pillar of salt. But Lot and his daughters were saved.

In this way, God remembered the promise made to Abraham. God destroyed the wicked people, but the good people God saved.

❏ Teaching the Story

Q: Why did God want to destroy the cities of Sodom and Gomorrah?
The people there were evil.

Q: Why did Abraham speak up about God's plan to destroy the cities?
Abraham did not want God to destroy the good people with the evil ones.

Q: When would God save the cities?
If God found ten good people, the cities would be saved.

Q: God remembered the promise made to Abraham. Who did God save from destruction?
God saved Lot and Lot's daughters.

❏ Vocabulary

faith belief and trust in God
justice fairness
innocent free from guilt or blame
pillar a column standing alone
wicked evil

> Abraham clearly shows his monotheistic faith here. He argues because he knows that the world God created is orderly and just, or can be made so. A pagan god, on the other hand, was thought to act on a whim and therefore could not be questioned.

Read More About It

"There is Only One," <u>Exploring Our Living Past</u>, p. 144. This rabbinic tale explores the origins of the monotheistic faith that is deduced by Abraham.

"Abraham Argues with God," <u>Lessons from Our Living Past</u>, p. 27. This selection offers another look at the conversation between God and Abraham in which Abraham wanted to make sure that God would not fail to be both just and merciful.

ABRAHAM AND SARAH

Activity Page

Mystery Word
For Readers: Today we call this great nation ISRAEL.
For Non-Readers: The children can find and cross out the letters that appear 4 times. Write the 6 remaining letters on the chalkboard and tell them the word.

Just By Looking
The answer is Path #2. Younger children can use colored pencils or crayons to see more easily which path leads to Canaan.

Good or Evil
There are four smiling faces in the group.

A Big Question
A class discussion focusing on this important question will help clarify the youngsters' understanding of behavior to be valued and emulated.

Let's Talk About It
What would you want so badly that you would even argue with God to get it?
Answers will vary. Abraham felt that God should not destroy good people with evil ones so he bargained with God.

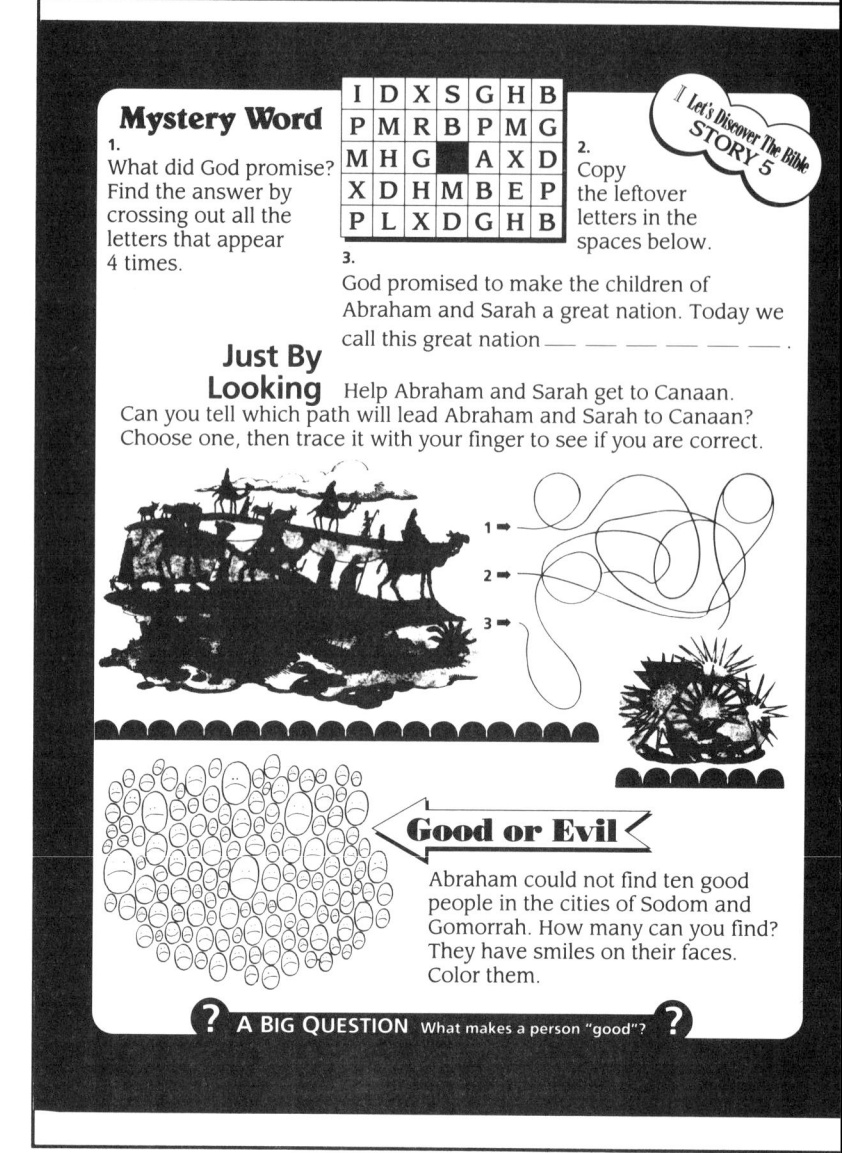

Mystery Word

1. What did God promise? Find the answer by crossing out all the letters that appear 4 times.

2. Copy the leftover letters in the spaces below.

3. God promised to make the children of Abraham and Sarah a great nation. Today we call this great nation ___ ___ ___ ___ ___ ___.

Just By Looking
Help Abraham and Sarah get to Canaan. Can you tell which path will lead Abraham and Sarah to Canaan? Choose one, then trace it with your finger to see if you are correct.

Good or Evil
Abraham could not find ten good people in the cities of Sodom and Gomorrah. How many can you find? They have smiles on their faces. Color them.

A BIG QUESTION What makes a person "good"?

Family Education

Learning at Home Distribute worksheet 5 at the end of class. Have the children bring home both the worksheet and the four-page folder containing the story of *Abraham and Sarah*.

Learning at Home worksheet available on page 77 in the back of this guide.

24 LET'S DISCOVER THE BIBLE

Isaac and Rebecca

When Sarah died, Abraham and Isaac missed her very much. Abraham was old. He knew that he too would soon die. Isaac needed a wife so that he would not be alone. Abraham said to his servant, "Go to the place I was born and find a wife for Isaac. Bring her to Isaac so that they can marry and have children of their own."

Abraham's servant took treasures of gold and silver and set out toward the city of Nahor. It was evening when he arrived, the time of day when the girls came down to the well to draw water. He made his camels sit by the well, and he prayed. "God of Abraham," he said, "choose a wife for Isaac. I will ask each of the girls to give me a drink. If one gives me a drink and then also waters my camels—I will know that she is the right girl for Isaac to marry."

❏ Motivation

Have the children stand in a circle and act out the people that you describe. Have everyone try each of the following: A sad person, a happy person, a tired person, a person who is thirsty, and someone who is surprised.

After they act out these roles, tell them that they will read about several different people and the feelings that they have at different times.

❏ Using the Illustration

Before they read the story, have the children examine the picture and tell what they think is happening in the story.

❏ Biblical Source

Genesis 24:1–67

❏ Background for the Teacher

The need to seek comfort in time of sorrow is addressed in the story of Isaac and Rebecca. Very often children do not understand death and how one copes with the loss of a loved one. However, they will understand being sad at losing something and that something else can replace that sadness.

The main part of the story focuses on the search by Abraham's servant for a bride for Isaac. Why does Abraham send his servant to the place where Abraham was born to find Isaac's new wife? Abraham wanted to find a woman who would be as special to Isaac as Sarah had been to him. The servant searches near the well, a theme that is repeated in other biblical stories.

❏ Vocabulary

servant a person who works in the service of another person
well a source of water

❏ Teaching the Story

Q: **Who did Abraham and Isaac miss?**
Abraham missed his wife, Sarah, who was Isaac's mother.

Q: **Abraham was old when Sarah died and he was worried that when he died, Isaac would be alone. What did Abraham do about his worries?**
He told his servant to find a wife for Isaac.

ISAAC AND REBECCA **25**

❑ Teaching the Story

Q: What did the girl do for the servant?
She gave him a drink of a water from her jar and she brought water from the well for the camels.

Q: The servant thanked God for choosing Rebecca. How did God choose Rebecca?
The servant had prayed to the God of Abraham to choose a wife for Isaac by having her pass a test, which Rebecca did.

Q: How was Rebecca related to Abraham?
Rebecca was the daughter of Bethuel, Abraham's nephew.

Q: How does Rebecca's father show the same kindness to the servant that Rebecca had shown at the well?
Rebecca's father welcomes the servant and feeds him and his camels.

Rebecca's repeated trips to the well for the servant and his camels was not an easy task. Rebecca probably had to descend a set of steep stairs leading down into a narrow pit, draw the water, and haul it back up the stairs many times. Clearly, it was a generous person who would do this for a stranger and his camels.

Just as he finished his prayer, a beautiful girl came and filled her jar with water. "I am very thirsty," the servant said. "Please let me drink a little water from your jar." And the girl answered, "Drink as much as you want. And I will also bring water for your camels." And she went back and forth to the well until every camel had finished drinking.

Then the girl said to the servant, "I am Rebecca, the daughter of Bethuel. Come to my home. You are tired, and we have room for a guest to spend the night." And Abraham's servant was surprised, for Bethuel was the nephew of Abraham. So the servant thanked God for choosing Rebecca.

At home, Rebecca's father welcomed the servant and fed his camels. He washed the dust of the desert from the servant's feet, and placed a meal on the table before him.

"I must tell you my tale before I eat," the servant said. "I was sent by your uncle Abraham to find a wife for his son Isaac." And the servant told all that had happened. He told how he prayed to find the right girl—one who was kind to all, to people and to animals. He told how he asked for a drink for himself, and Rebecca gave him a drink and also watered his camels. He told how Rebecca invited him home for the night. And he told how he discovered that Rebecca was part of Abraham's family.

Hands-on Learning

Rebecca's Test The object of this game is for Rebecca to deliver the most water to the servant and his camels. Divide the class into groups of four students per team. One person on the team will be Rebecca, another will be the servant, and two others will be camels. (You can have more or less camels depending on class size.)

If you can play the game outside, set up a large bucket of water at one end of the playing area. Otherwise you can use a substitute for the water—styrofoam packing peanuts, dry cereal, or raw rice or macaroni will work

26 LET'S DISCOVER THE BIBLE

At last he said, "I have brought presents of gold and silver for your family. Let Rebecca come and be a wife for Isaac, the son of Abraham."

The next morning, they called Rebecca and asked, "Do you wish to go with this man to become the wife of Isaac?" And she said, "I will go with him." And they blessed Rebecca and bid her farewell.

Then Rebecca mounted a camel and she rode with Abraham's servant back to the Promised Land.

Isaac went for a walk one evening. He looked up and, behold, he saw the camels coming toward him. Just then, Rebecca looked out and saw Isaac. "Who is that man coming to welcome us?" she asked the servant. And the servant answered, "That is Isaac, my master."

Isaac and Rebecca fell in love at once. Isaac took Rebecca to the tent that had belonged to Sarah, his mother. And Rebecca became his wife, bringing him children and comfort after the death of his mother.

❑ Teaching the Story

Q: **What did the servant bring for Rebecca's family?**
The servant gave a gift of gold and silver from Abraham.

Q: **What happened when Isaac and Rebecca met each other?**
They fell in love.

❑ Vocabulary

behold look at
master the servant's boss

Read More About It

"A Wife for Isaac," *Stories from Our Living Past*, p. 80. In this adaptation, Abraham's servant, Eliezer, must find a wife for Isaac without "judging a book by its cover."

fine. Give every team member a cup. Rebecca must run to the well (the bucket), fill a small cup of water, run back to her team, and dump the water into the servant's cup. Then she should return to the well to fill the camel's cups. The first team to have all of its cups filled is the winner.

Activity Page

What Is Hidden?
For Readers: REBECCA
For Non-Readers: The children can color in the 7 letters. Write them on the chalkboard and read the name for the class.

Look Look Look
This exercise will develop visual perception and attention to detail.

Opposites
For Readers: OLD, FIND, RIGHT, GIRL, WIFE
For Non-Readers: Complete the exercise orally, writing responses on the chalkboard.

A Big Question
A class discussion focusing on this important question should encourage specific examples of kindness experienced by the children.

Let's Talk About It

How did Isaac overcome the sadness he felt after the death of Sarah, his mother?
Abraham realized that Isaac would be lonely so he arranged for Isaac to get married. Although Isaac would never again have his mother, with Rebecca he would not be lonely.

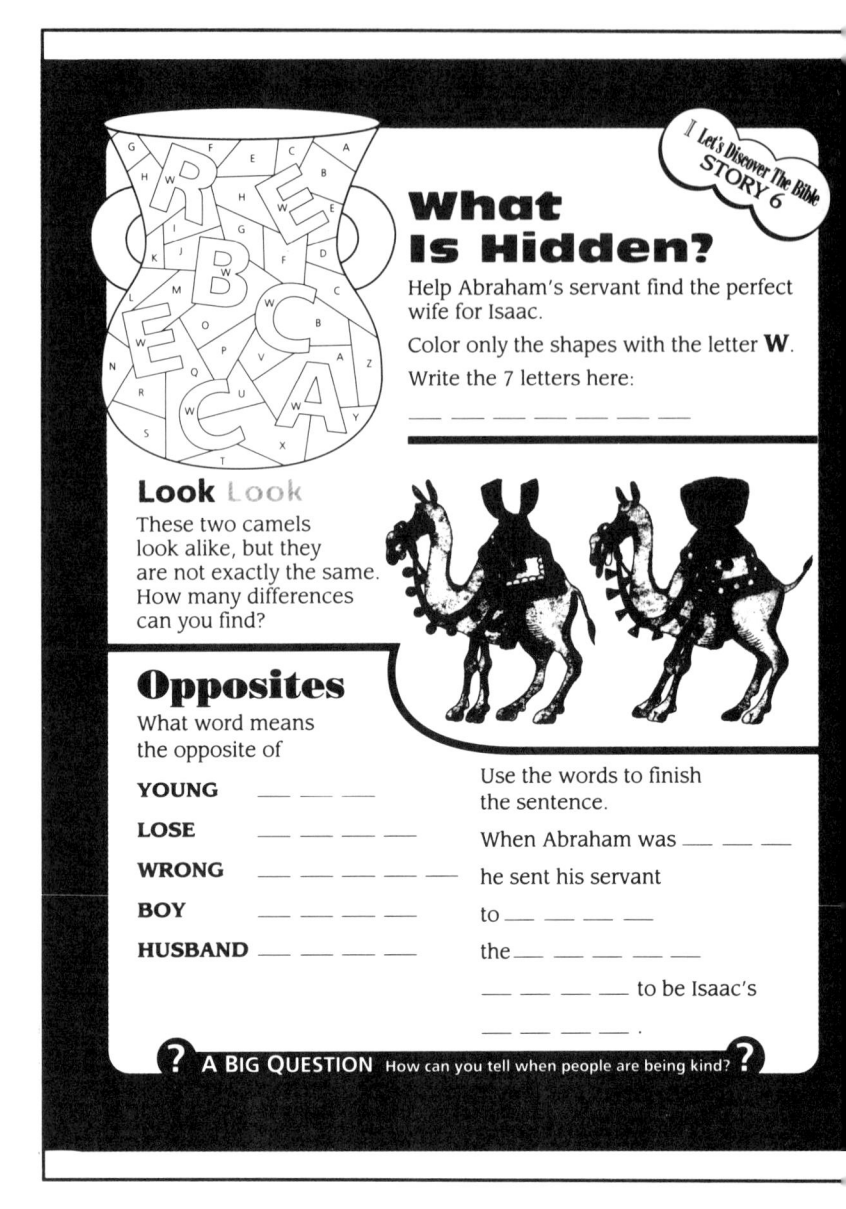

What Is Hidden?

Help Abraham's servant find the perfect wife for Isaac.
Color only the shapes with the letter **W**.
Write the 7 letters here:

_ _ _ _ _ _ _

Look Look
These two camels look alike, but they are not exactly the same. How many differences can you find?

Opposites
What word means the opposite of

YOUNG _ _ _
LOSE   _ _ _ _
WRONG _ _ _ _ _
BOY   _ _ _
HUSBAND _ _ _ _

Use the words to finish the sentence.

When Abraham was _ _ _ he sent his servant to _ _ _ _ the _ _ _ _ _ _ _ _ _ to be Isaac's _ _ _ _.

A BIG QUESTION How can you tell when people are being kind?

❏ Classroom Enrichment (Optional)

Duplicate and distribute worksheet 6. Allow the children to color in the picture. Paste each picture onto a cardboard backing. After the glue dries, cut the picture along the dotted lines and let the children piece together their puzzles.

Enrichment worksheet available on page 79 in the back of this guide.

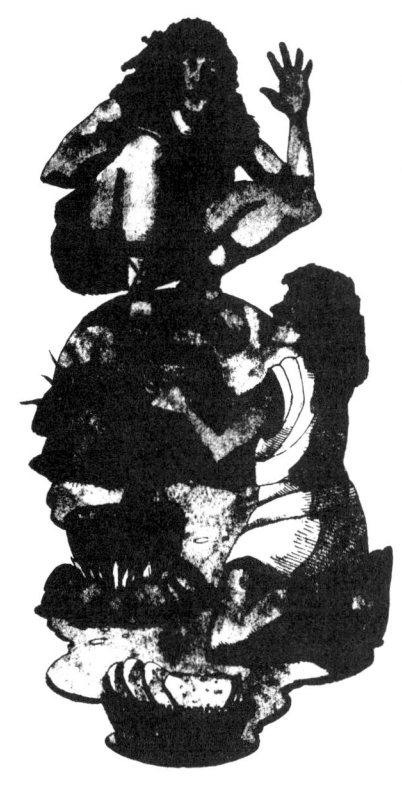

Jacob and Esau

Isaac and Rebecca had twin sons, Esau and Jacob. Esau was the older and loved to hunt in the fields. Esau was Isaac's favorite son. But Rebecca loved Jacob more because Jacob stayed close to home, helping his mother.

One time, Esau came home very hungry after hunting all day. Jacob was cooking a stew, and Esau said, "Give me some of that red stuff quickly, or I shall die!"

Jacob asked, "What will you give me if I feed you now?"

"I will sell you whatever you want in exchange for a bowl of stew," said Esau.

"Sell me the special blessing due to the oldest son," said Jacob. And Esau answered, "Why not? What good is the special blessing when I am so hungry?" And Esau sold his blessing to Jacob.

❑ Motivation

This story introduces a third generation after Abraham. A key theme is the importance of the inheritance of this lineage. To develop the idea of lineage, have your students create a family tree. Allow them to include many relatives, but the minimum should include their parents and any siblings they have.

❑ Biblical Source

Genesis 25–27

❑ Background for the Teacher

Does Esau get the better deal when he sells his birthright for a bowl of stew? Esau cares more for the present than the future, thus, satisfying a craving is more fulfilling to him than a promise of future property. Like the birthright, Jacob takes the special blessing because he would be the future leader of the Jewish people, following the tradition of Abraham and Isaac.

❑ Using the Illustration

After reading the front page, have the children look at the illustration and identify which boy is Jacob and which one is Esau. Ask them to identify the sentences in the text that helped them identify the characters in the illustration.

❑ Teaching the Story

Q: Which son was Isaac's favorite?
Isaac favored Esau.

Q: Which son was Rebecca's favorite?
Rebecca favored Jacob.

Q: What did Esau sell to Jacob for a bowl of stew?
Esau sold his birthright.

❑ Vocabulary

exchange trade, swap
birthright a possession that a person is entitled to by birth

❏ Teaching the Story

Q: What did Isaac ask of Esau?
Isaac wants a last meal of freshly-hunted meat.

Q: Why does Rebecca want Jacob to bring the meal to Isaac?
Rebecca wants Jacob to receive his father's blessing.

Q: If Isaac is blind, how can he tell his sons apart?
Isaac can distinguish between the two because Esau's arms are hairy and Jacob's are smooth.

Q: How does Rebecca overcome the difference in appearance between Jacob and Esau?
She has Jacob wear Esau's clothes and goatskin on his arms.

The Bible does not say that Isaac was blind, only that his eyes had become too dim to see. This could mean that he could not see which son would best carry on the traditions of Abraham.

In time, Isaac grew old and blind. He called Esau to his bedside. Isaac said, "Soon I am going to die. Before that, I would like to eat a meal of freshly-hunted meat. If you will fix this meal for me, I will give you the blessing of the oldest son." So Esau went hunting for meat for his father.

But Rebecca overheard what Isaac said. She called Jacob to her and said, "Do as I tell you, and the blessing of the oldest son will be yours!" Jacob did all that his mother asked. He brought two young goats to her and she cooked them the way Isaac liked. Then she said, "Take this to your father to eat, and he will bless you."

"No," said Jacob. "Father knows that Esau has hairy arms and my arms are smooth. Father cannot see, but if he touches me to bless me, he will know that it is a trick and he will curse me instead."

"I have thought of that," Rebecca said. And she gave Jacob some of Esau's clothes to wear. And she covered Jacob's arms and hands with the rough skin of the goats she had cooked. Then she gave Jacob the food for his father and sent him in to Isaac.

❏ Displaying a Family Tree

To show the children how we are all descended from Abraham, create a large family tree on a bulletin board with Abraham and Sarah at the base, Isaac and Rebecca above them and Jacob and Esau as branches. As the class reads additional Bible stories, add more names to the tree. Add your student's family trees, from the motivation activity on page 29, to the highest branches of the trees.

Jacob said to his father, "Here is the meal you wanted. Come and eat, then give me your special blessing."

Isaac said, "Come closer, my son. Let me feel you. Then I will know that you are truly Esau." Jacob came closer. And Isaac felt his arms and hands and was confused.

"The voice sounds like the voice of Jacob," Isaac thought. "But these are surely the hands of Esau!"

In the end, Isaac ate and drank. When he finished eating, he gave Jacob the special blessing of the first-born and Jacob left.

A moment later, Esau came back from his hunt. He too cooked a meal and brought it to his father. Suddenly Isaac knew that Jacob had fooled him.

Esau said, "Bless me, my father." But Isaac said, "I have given the special blessing to Jacob, and it cannot be given again even though he tricked me! Yet I will give you another blessing. You too will grow into a great nation."

And that is what happened. Esau became the father of many peoples. And Jacob's sons became the Twelve Tribes of Israel, the Jewish people.

❏ Teaching the Story

Q: Did Rebecca and Jacob trick Isaac?
Yes, Isaac gave his blessing to Jacob instead of Esau.

Q: Why couldn't Isaac also give the blessing to Esau?
The blessing could only be given once, even if Isaac had been tricked.

Q: What did Jacob's sons become?
Jacob's sons became the Twelve Tribes of Israel, the Jewish people.

❏ Using the Illustration

Have the class look at the illustration and have several volunteers each make a statement about what is taking place.

Read More About It

"Jacob's Dream," Exploring Our Living Past, p. 153. In Jacob's dream God reaffirms the covenant with Abraham as it continues with his descendant, Jacob.

Hands-on Learning

Divide the class into groups of three students. In each group, have one student put on a blindfold and try to identify each of the other two members of the group by only touching their arms. Those two students should try to trick the blindfolded one. Have each group member take a turn being blindfolded.

Activity Page

Picture Story

For Readers: Isaac and Rebecca had twin sons, Esau and Jacob. Esau sold his birthright to Jacob for a bowl of stew.

For Non-Readers: The children can "read" the pictures as you say the words.

Who's Talking?

1-Esau 2-Jacob 3-Rebecca 4-Isaac
Ask the children to try and sound like the characters in the story as they say each statement.

Think About It

What is so important to you that you would never sell it?

A Riddle

Isaac gave Jacob the special BLESSING.

A Big Question

A class discussion focusing on this question should encourage specific examples of the important things that parents do for their children.

Let's Talk About It

Is the oldest child in every family always the favorite one?

Answers will vary. Discuss how everyone in every family is special in their own way. Mention how God chose Jacob to lead the Twelve Tribes of Israel although he was not the first born.

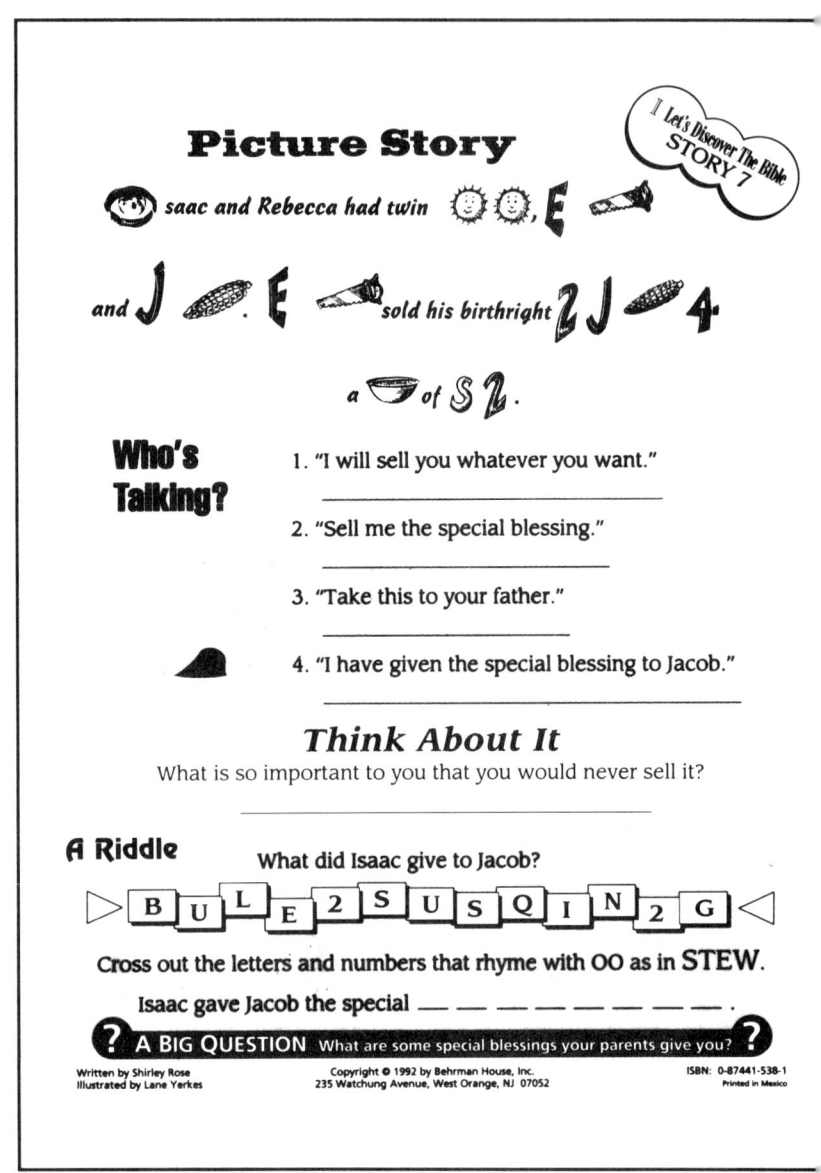

❏ Classroom Enrichment

Esau thought that a meal today was more important than his birthright tomorrow. Have a discussion with the class to promote the value that we must prepare for the future today. Discuss what people need today and what they need to do today for the future.

32 LET'S DISCOVER THE BIBLE

Joseph and His Brothers

Jacob was called by two names—Jacob and Israel. He had twelve sons and they were called the Children of Israel. Most of his sons spent their days taking care of the goats. But Joseph was Jacob's favorite, and Jacob took special care of him. Indeed, one day Jacob gave Joseph a wonderful gift—a coat striped with colors, the kind of coat that kings wore.

Now Joseph's brothers were jealous of Joseph and his marvelous coat. They said, "Let's kill him. We can say that a wild animal ate Joseph." But Reuben, the oldest brother, said, "No. Let's just throw him into a deep hole." And Reuben thought, "Later tonight, I will return and rescue Joseph." When Joseph came to see his brothers, they grabbed him and threw him into a hole so deep that he could not climb out.

❑ Motivation

Write the vocabulary term *jealous* on the chalkboard and ask the class for a definition of the word. Have them talk about times when they were jealous. Ask what made them jealous. If anyone talks about jealousy between siblings, remind them of the story of Jacob and Esau when a parent, playing favorites, caused a problem. Tell them that in the story they are about to read, jealousy between brothers leads to trouble.

❑ Biblical Source

Genesis 35–47

❑ Background for the Teacher

Once again, here is a story which focuses on the consequences of playing favorites with children. Joseph's brothers were jealous of Joseph and the special treatment he received from their father, Jacob. The focus of the story, as it begins, is that envy and jealousy can have dangerous results. By the end of the story, the focus shifts to the brothers repentance and Joseph's forgiveness.

The last 14 chapters in the book of Genesis are devoted to the story of Joseph and his brothers. Take the time to read this well-told story. It will provide you with detail to enhance your student's abbreviated version.

❑ Teaching the Story

Q: What is Jacob's other name?
He is also known as Israel.

Q: Who was Jacob's favorite son?
His favorite was Joseph.

Q: Why were Joseph's brothers jealous of him?
They were jealous of the treatment Joseph received from their father and they envied his new coat.

Q: What did Joseph's brothers do to him?
They threw him into a deep hole.

❑ Vocabulary

jealous feelings of resentment towards a rival

❑ Teaching the Story

Q: What did Joseph's brothers do to him?
They sold Joseph into slavery.

Q: To where was Joseph taken?
He was taken to Egypt.

Q: What did Joseph say Pharaoh's dream meant?
Joseph explained that seven good years would be followed by seven lean years.

Q: What did Joseph do to prepare for the seven lean years?
During the seven good years, he put the grain into storehouses to keep it fresh.

❑ Vocabulary

traders traveling merchants
Pharaoh title of an Egyptian ruler, king; often addressed by this name
harvest a ripe crop

You may want to read aloud to your class the Pharaoh's dream. It is in Genesis, Chapter 14.

Just then, they heard the jingling of camel bells. A group of traders was passing by on the way to Egypt. Judah said, "Let's sell Joseph to them!" And they did. Then they told their father that Joseph was dead, and Jacob cried bitter tears for his lost son. And the traders took Joseph to Egypt where they sold him into slavery.

One night, Pharaoh, the king of Egypt, had a dream. None of his wise men could tell him what it meant. But one of the servants said, "There is a man called Joseph in your prison. He can tell you what your dream means." So Pharaoh sent for Joseph and Joseph explained the dream. "There will be seven good years," said Joseph, "followed by seven years of hunger." Then Pharaoh said, "Your God has given you wisdom. From now on, you and I will rule Egypt together."

Seven years passed. The harvests were good and Joseph put the grain in big storehouses to keep it fresh. Then came seven years of bad crops, and the people were hungry. But Joseph opened the storehouses and gave out food so that the people would not starve.

In those years, all the world came to Egypt to buy food. Jacob and his sons also needed food. One day, Jacob said to his sons, "Go to Egypt and buy food so that we may live." And the brothers saddled their donkeys and left.

Hands-on Learning

Sequencing Divide the class into six groups. Provide each group with construction paper and the art supplies they will need to illustrate one scene from the story. Assign the following scenes:
   Joseph in his striped coat
   Joseph in the pit
   Joseph being sold into slavery
   Joseph interpreting Pharaoh's dream
   His brothers journey to Egypt
   Joseph revealing his identity to his brothers
Collect the illustrations and display them in a scrambled order. Have the children put them in the correct order.

34 LET'S DISCOVER THE BIBLE

The brothers were taken to see Joseph. Many years had passed and Joseph had changed. They did not know that the man they were speaking to was their own brother. Yet Joseph knew them at once. "How many brothers do you have?" he asked them. And they answered, "Our father had twelve sons, but one is dead and we are very sorry for that."

Suddenly Joseph stood up and said, "Do not be sad any longer! I am your brother, Joseph! You sold me into slavery. But really it was God sending me ahead to save many people from dying of hunger."

Then the brothers returned home with food in their sacks and joy in their hearts. They said to Jacob, "Joseph is alive! He rules over Egypt! He wants all of us to join him and live there."

And that is how the Children of Israel came to live in the land of Egypt.

❏ Teaching the Story

Q: Did Joseph's brothers recognize him when they spoke to him?
No.

Q: What were they sorry about?
They were sorry for having sold their brother into slavery.

Q: What did Joseph believe God had done?
Joseph believed that God had sent Joseph to Egypt to save many people from dying of hunger.

❏ Using the Illustration

Have the children compare the illustration on this page and the one on the first page. How has Joseph's appearance changed? How have the roles changed between Joseph and his brothers? How have their feelings towards each other changed?

Read More About It

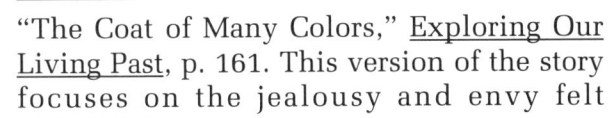

"The Coat of Many Colors," <u>Exploring Our Living Past</u>, p. 161. This version of the story focuses on the jealousy and envy felt towards Joseph by his brothers.

"Joseph Sees His Brothers Again," <u>Exploring Our Living Past</u>, p. 169. This offers the conclusion to the story when Joseph, who is now a member of the Egyptian court, tests and later forgives his brothers.

Activity Page

Maze
Children always enjoy mazes and readers and non-readers alike will be able to complete this activity.

Color By Number
You may have to assist children who can not yet read with the number/color code.

Understanding the Story
Why were the brothers jealous of Joseph?
   They envied his new coat and the treatment he received from their father.
What did the brothers do to Joseph?
   They sold Joseph into slavery.
What did Joseph do in Egypt?
   He interpreted the Pharaoh's dream and helped prepare for the lean years.
What happened when the brothers came to Egypt?
   They were reunited with Joseph.

A Big Question
A class discussion focusing on this question should include examples of sharing and not sharing experienced by the children.

Let's Talk About It
Why is it important to forgive when others have hurt us? Why not take revenge?
Answers will vary. Joseph forgave his brothers because he found that God had given purpose to his being sent to Egypt. Their answers may include that two wrongs don't make a right.

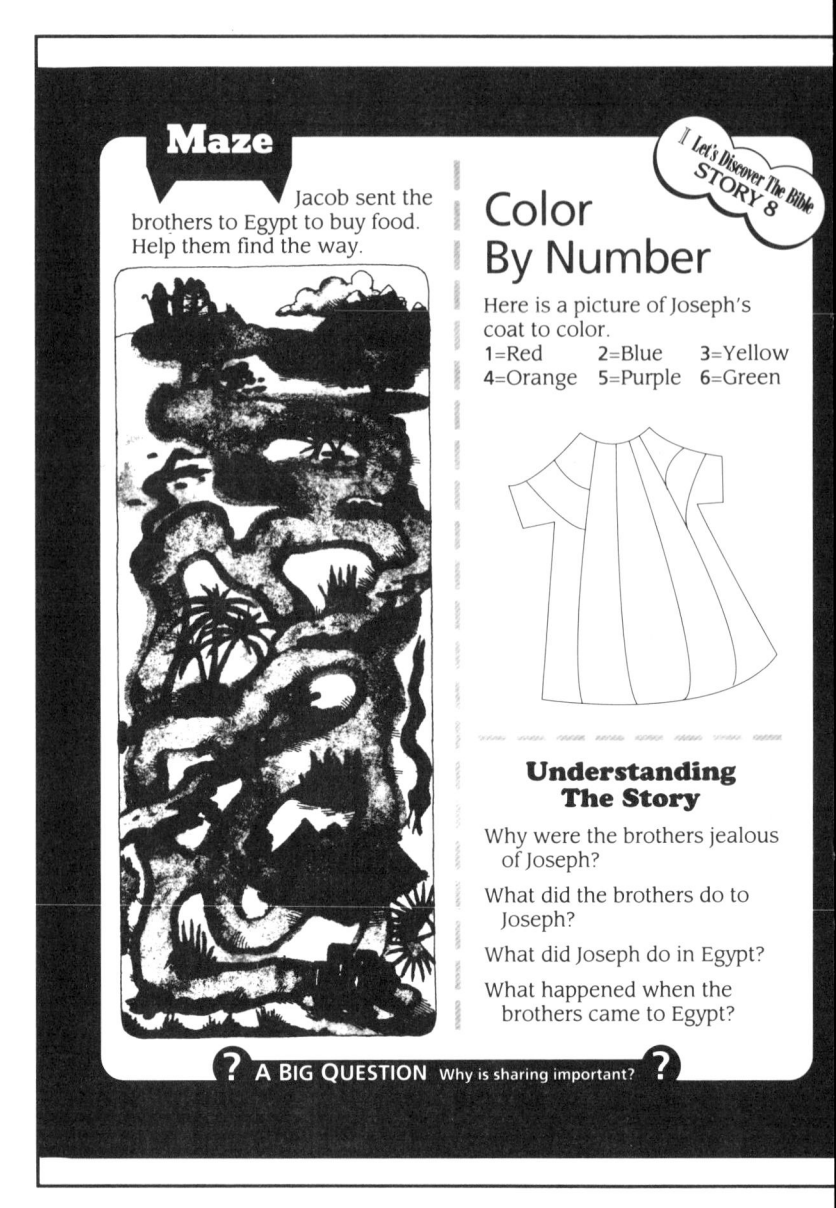

Maze
Jacob sent the brothers to Egypt to buy food. Help them find the way.

Color By Number
Let's Discover The Bible STORY 8

Here is a picture of Joseph's coat to color.
1=Red 2=Blue 3=Yellow
4=Orange 5=Purple 6=Green

Understanding The Story
Why were the brothers jealous of Joseph?

What did the brothers do to Joseph?

What did Joseph do in Egypt?

What happened when the brothers came to Egypt?

? A BIG QUESTION Why is sharing important? **?**

❏ Classroom Enrichment (Optional)
Duplicate and distribute worksheet 8 to the class. Have them unscramble the names of Joseph's brothers.

Enrichment worksheet available on page 81 in the back of this guide.

Baby Moses

The Children of Israel lived in Egypt for many years. They grew into a mighty nation. At last, Pharaoh the king said, "These people called Israel are too strong. One day they will make war against us and kill us. Let us make them our slaves."

So Pharaoh forced the Israelites to make bricks and to build cities. Yet the harder they worked, the stronger they became. And Pharaoh was frightened. "We must do something to make them weaker," he said. "I command that if they give birth to a baby girl, she shall live. But if they give birth to a baby boy, he shall be drowned in the River Nile!"

❏ Motivation

Ask your students to tell how their family shows that they love them. How do they show that they love their parents? Explain that they will read about one mother who was willing to give up her child because of how much she loved him.

❏ Biblical Source

Exodus 1–2:10

❏ Background for the Teacher

Generations pass between the time of Joseph and the baby, Moses. The time lapse must occur because Joseph's immediate descendants were part of the Egyptian aristocracy and would not easily become slaves. The treatment of the Israelites by Pharaoh sets the stage for the development of one of the most important stories in Judaism. And yet, this story of the baby Moses seems to be told for the purpose of explaining the origin of his name—an Egyptian name—given to him by his adoptive mother.

❏ Using the Illustration

Ask your class: What is the man on the left doing? (He is ordering the Israelites to put their male babies into the river.) Have your students describe the emotion being felt by the people holding the baby. (scared, nervous, worried, etc.)

❏ Teaching the Story

Q: Why did Pharaoh force the Children of Israel into slavery?
He feared that they would make war upon the Egyptians.

Q: What job were the Israelites forced to do?
They were forced to make bricks and to build cities.

Q: As the Israelites became stronger, how did Pharaoh want to weaken them?
Pharaoh ordered that all baby boys must be drowned in the river.

BABY MOSES **37**

❑ Teaching the Story

Q: What was the mother's plan to save her child?
She made a basket of reeds, waterproofed it with tar, and set her baby afloat in the river.

Q: Who was sent to watch the basket?
The baby's sister, Miriam, was sent to watch the basket.

Q: Who discovered the baby in the basket?
The daughter of Pharaoh found the baby.

❑ Vocabulary

woe great suffering from misfortune or trouble

reeds various tall slender grasses (as bamboo) of wet areas that have large stems with large joints; a growth or mass of reeds

Show the class a map of Egypt which illustrates the location of the Nile River.

In these sad times, a baby boy was born to an Israelite couple. The father cried, "Woe to us. It is a son. Now our baby will be drowned." But the mother said, "Do not worry. I have a plan to save him."

The mother took reeds from the river and wove a basket. She took sticky black tar and covered the basket inside and out. She placed her baby son in the basket and carried him down to the river. There she set the basket out to float in the water.

The mother said to her daughter, Miriam, "Watch what happens to the basket. Come back and tell me." And Miriam walked along beside the river, watching the basket, wondering what would happen to her baby brother.

It was afternoon. The daughter of Pharaoh came out of the palace to bathe in the river. Just as she came to the river's edge, she saw a basket floating toward her. She was curious and she bent over to look. She could hardly believe her eyes. There was a baby!

Hands-on Learning

Duplicate worksheet 9. Make one copy for each student. Cut the worksheet along the dotted lines to separate the 4 pictures of baby Moses, the Pharaoh, his daughter, and the Hebrew slaves. Place the pictures in a bag and shake them up.

Have one student draw one picture out of the bag. If the student doesn't have that picture, they place it face up in front of them; the next child then takes a turn.

Hands-on Learning worksheet available on page 83 in the back of this guide.

38   LET'S DISCOVER THE BIBLE

Miriam watched as Pharaoh's daughter picked up the baby and cradled it in her arms. "I know this is a child of the Israelites," the Pharaoh's daughter said. "But he is so beautiful, I will keep him as my own."

Then Miriam came out of hiding. "Princess," she said, "I know a woman among the Israelites who can be your baby's nurse."

And the princess said, "Bring the woman to the palace. She will raise my baby for me."

Then Miriam went home and told her mother all that had happened. She took her mother to the palace, and Pharaoh's daughter said, "Take the child. Care for him and feed him. When he is older bring him back to me. Be careful with him, for he is now a prince of Egypt!"

So the baby was saved from drowning. And Pharaoh's daughter named the baby *Moses*, which means "pulled from the water." And Moses grew up straight and strong—a child of Israel and a prince of Egypt.

❑ Teaching the Story

Q: How does Miriam get her mother to take care of her own baby?
Miriam gets the Pharaoh's daughter to hire Miriam's mother as a nurse.

Q: What does the name Moses mean?
"Moses" means "pulled from the water".

❑ Vocabulary

nurse a person who has the care of a young child

❑ Using the Illustration

Ask questions about the story by using the illustration.
   Who is hiding in the reeds? *(Miriam)*
   Who is the woman kneeling at the water's edge? *(Pharaoh's daughter)*
   Who is in the basket? *(Moses)*
   Who made the basket and placed Moses in it? *(his mother)*
   What was she protecting him from? *(The Pharaoh's order to drown all baby boys)*

If a student draws a picture that they already have, then the picture is put back into the bag, and the next student takes a turn.

If a Pharaoh is drawn, they put it back in the bag, and lose their turn.

Play continues in this manner by all. The first one to collect all three pictures—baby Moses, the Pharaoh's daughter, and the Hebrew slaves—wins.

Activity Page

Follow the Dots
Readers and non-readers will enjoy discovering the picture.

Hidden Letters
For Non-Readers: Read the question aloud to get the answer *Pharaoh*.

Mystery Word
For Readers: By reading the letters from left to right, top line first, the answer, MIRIAM, will appear.
For Non-Readers: Sound out all of the letters to arrive at the solution.

A Big Question
As the class discusses the question, ask the children about babies in their family.

Follow the Dots
Connect the dots to finish the picture.

Hidden Letters
Draw a straight line from A to B.
Then draw another line from C to D.

Color the 7 letters **BLACK**. Who was the king of Egypt?

Mystery Word
Cross out every letter that rhymes with the sound **BEE** as in **BABY**.

E	M	P	I	R
G	Z	I	C	D
A	T	E	V	M

_ _ _ _ _ _ was Moses' sister.

A BIG QUESTION Why do we have to take special care of babies?

Let's Talk About It

How does the Bible treat the subject of slavery?

Answers will vary but should focus on the cruel treatment experienced by the Israelites in Egypt. Responses may include reference to the story of Joseph. His slavery was a cruel fate.

40 LET'S DISCOVER THE BIBLE

Let My People Go

Moses turned aside. Something on the mountain had caught his eye. It was a bush blazing with fire. But the fire was not hurting the bush. As Moses stared at the strange sight, God's voice seemed to come from the burning bush. God said, "I have heard the Children of Israel crying because they are slaves. Go back to Egypt. Tell Pharaoh to let My people go."

Moses returned to Egypt. He and his brother Aaron went to Pharaoh the king. They said, "The God of Israel commands, 'Let My people go so they may worship Me.'" But Pharaoh answered, "I will not let them go!" Instead, Pharaoh made the work of the Hebrew slaves even harder than before.

❑ Biblical Source

Exodus 5–12:51

❑ Background for the Teacher

The Torah does not tell about Moses' childhood except for the story of Moses as a baby. This gap is filled by the Midrash. In Exodus, Moses has grown up and sees the labor of his kinsmen. He sees an Egyptian kill a Hebrew so he kills the Egyptian. Fearing Pharaoh's rage, Moses flees. He arrives in the land of Midian. Like the story of Isaac and Rebecca, Moses shows kindness by helping to water the animals and is rewarded with the hospitality of the priest of Midian. The Priest marries his daughter Zipporah to Moses. They have a son, Gershom, and Moses has settled in the land of Midian. But God hears the suffering of the children of Israel and will call upon Moses to deliver them.

❑ Teaching the Story

Q: What was unusual about the burning bush?
The bush was on fire, but the fire was not hurting the bush.

Q: Moses hears God's voice. What does the voice tell Moses to do?
Moses must go back to Egypt to tell Pharaoh to let the Israelites go.

❑ Motivation

Your students probably know this story better than all others because of the Passover Seder. Find out what they already know about the story. Ask about the significance of the symbols of Passover—matzah, maror, and so on.

❑ Using the Illustration

Point out the rod in Moses' hand. Explain to your class that Moses was a reluctant leader. He feared that people would not believe that the Lord had appeared before him. He also pleaded with God to send someone else because Moses was "slow of speech and of a slow tongue." God tells Moses that his brother, Aaron, will speak for him and that Aaron will use the rod to display God's signs.

❑ **Teaching the Story**

Q: What would God do until Pharaoh lets the people go?
God will bring plagues upon Egypt.

Q: What plagues were brought on Egypt?
The river turned to blood; frogs, flies, and insects swarmed over the land; their cattle died and their skin blistered; hailstones fell; locusts filled the sky; and there were three days of darkness.

Q: What happened after each plague?
Pharaoh still refused to let the Israelites go.

❑ **Vocabulary**

plague a disastrous occasion
blister a raised area of the outer skin containing watery liquid often caused by a burn
locust a grasshopper that often migrates in vast swarms and eats up the plants in its course

---

List the plagues on the chalkboard as you read them. To learn the ten plagues, use the same sequencing Hands-on Learning activity described on page 34.

God said, "Terrible things will happen in Egypt. I will bring plagues to the land, until Pharaoh lets My people go."

Aaron struck the river with his rod and the water turned red as blood. Pharaoh laughed. "It's the trick of a magician," he said. Then Aaron stretched out his rod and frogs were everywhere, leaping and croaking. Pharaoh said, "Tell your God to kill the frogs and I will let your people go." But when the frogs disappeared, Pharaoh changed his mind.

Next, God sent gnats—tiny flies that filled the air like a fog. Then came bigger insects. Again Pharaoh promised to let the Israelites go, if God would remove the insects from the air. But when the insects were gone, Pharaoh changed his mind once again.

The fifth plague killed the Egyptians' cattle. The sixth plague brought blisters and sores to the Egyptians' skin. Then God sent a mighty thunderstorm and heavy hailstones fell, battering people and animals alike. Yet, no hail fell on the streets of the Hebrews. Pharaoh said, "If your God will stop the hail, I will let your people go." But as soon as the hail stopped, Pharaoh's heart grew as hard as a hailstone, and he refused to let the Israelites go.

God sent swarms of locusts to eat the grain and the trees. They filled the skies like a black cloud. They came through doors and windows into the rooms of the Egyptian houses. Then came the darkness—three full days without light. Still Pharaoh would not let the Israelites go.

Hands-on Learning

Passover Haggadah As you read through the stories of Moses and the deliverance from slavery in Egypt, the children can make their own Haggadahs. Each child will need 18" x 24" construction paper for a cover and white drawing paper of the same size for the inside pages. First, cut all paper to 18" x 12" size. Then fold the paper in half to have pages that are 9" x 12" in size.

Moses warned Pharaoh, "If you will not let the Israelites go, God will send one more plague, the most terrible of all. The first-born of every Egyptian family will die!" But Pharaoh would not listen.

Then God said, "Tell the Children of Israel to make a Passover feast. Tell them to put lamb's blood on their doorposts. The angel of death will see the blood and pass over any house marked with it."

It came to pass at midnight, that God sent the tenth plague, killing the first-born of every family in Egypt—even killing Pharaoh's oldest son. At last Pharaoh said, "Take your people and go." And the Children of Israel did not even wait for the dough of their bread to rise. They just gathered quickly and followed Moses out of the land of Egypt.

Let the children decorate the cover using crayons, felt-tip markers, or other art supplies. Next, they can draw scenes from the story on the inside pages. Begin with the baby Moses and include the burning bush, the ten plagues, and the contents of the next story, Moses on the Mountain. Staple the white paper inside the construction paper cover. Display the haggadot in a prominent place.

❏ Teaching the Story

Q: What was the last and most terrible plague?
The tenth plague was the killing of the first-born of every family of Egypt.

Q: How did the children of Israel tell the angel of death to pass over their homes?
They put lamb's blood on their door posts.

Q: How did Pharaoh respond to the tenth plague?
He told the Israelites to go out of Egypt.

Q: What happened because the Children of Israel left so quickly?
The dough of their bread did not have enough time to rise.

Read More About It

"The Crown of Pharaoh," <u>Exploring Our Living Past</u>, p. 178. Because the Bible skips the childhood of Moses in the Pharaoh's court, the Midrash fills in the gaps. This tale helps to explain why Moses had difficulty with his speech.

"Moses and the Lost Lamb," <u>Stories from Our Living Past</u>, p. 76. This story from the Midrash shows that Moses cares so much for his flock of sheep that he would make an excellent shepherd for his people, Israel.

LET MY PEOPLE GO

Activity Page

Decode the Message
For Readers: LET MY PEOPLE GO

For Non-Readers: Ask the children what Moses told Pharaoh.

First-Letter Game
For Non-Readers: Write the letters on the board and read the name AARON to the class.

Opposites
For Readers: KING, GO, NO, TERRIBLE, OUT

For Non-Readers: Conduct the activity aloud.

A Big Question
Class discussion may focus on God making the people of Israel God's chosen people.

When you reach the end of the story, you may want to give out matzah as an appropriate snack.

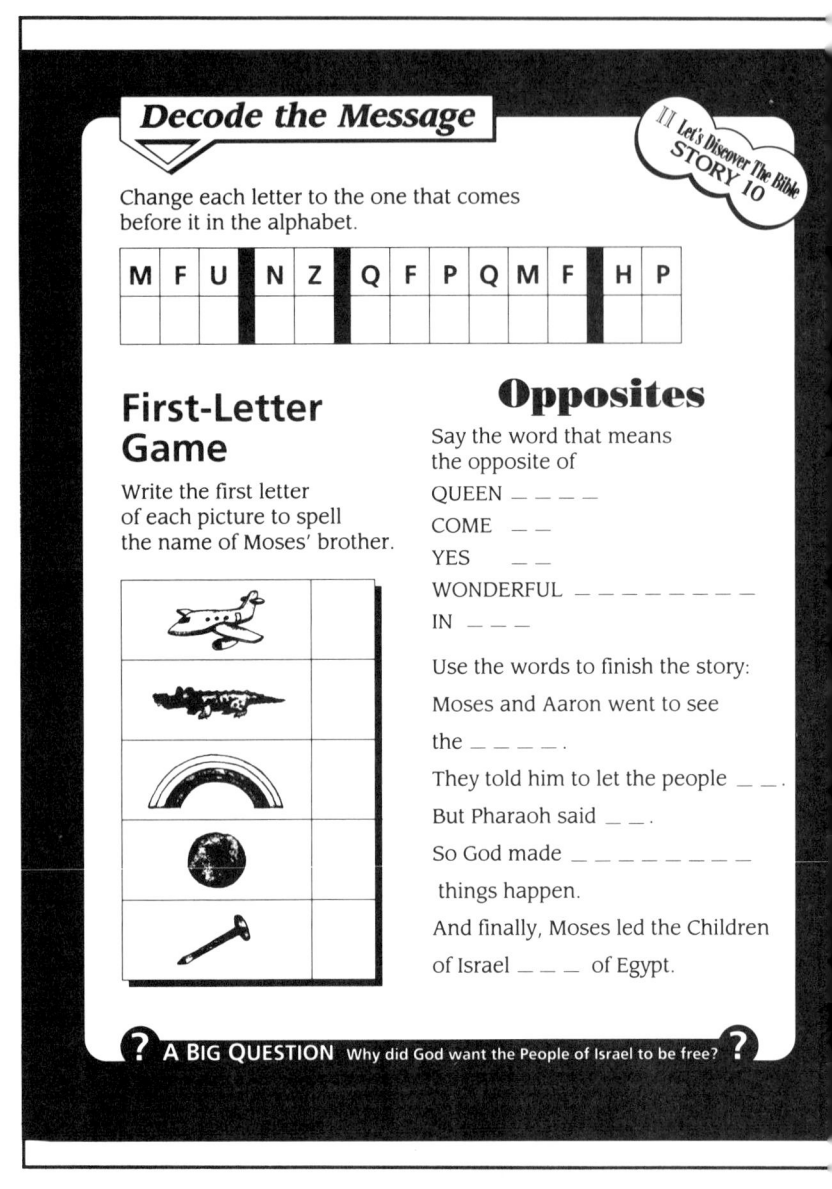

Decode the Message

Change each letter to the one that comes before it in the alphabet.

M	F	U	N	Z	Q	F	P	Q	M	F	H	P

Let's Discover The Bible STORY 10

First-Letter Game

Write the first letter of each picture to spell the name of Moses' brother.

Opposites

Say the word that means the opposite of

QUEEN _ _ _ _
COME _ _
YES _ _
WONDERFUL _ _ _ _ _ _ _ _
IN _ _ _

Use the words to finish the story:

Moses and Aaron went to see the _ _ _ _ _.

They told him to let the people _ _.

But Pharaoh said _ _.

So God made _ _ _ _ _ _ _ _ things happen.

And finally, Moses led the Children of Israel _ _ _ of Egypt.

? A BIG QUESTION Why did God want the People of Israel to be free? **?**

Let's Talk About It

Why was Moses chosen by God to go before Pharaoh?

Answers will vary. Point out that Moses grew up in the royal court and would be prepared to meet with a Pharaoh.

❑ Classroom Enrichment (Optional)

Duplicate and distribute worksheet 10. Have the children find all of the ten plagues in the word search.

Enrichment worksheet available on page 85 in the back of this guide.

44 LET'S DISCOVER THE BIBLE

Moses on the Mountain

Moses led the Children of Israel out of Egypt and they camped by the Sea of Reeds. Meanwhile, Pharaoh said, "Let us bring the slaves back." So all the chariots of the army of Egypt chased after the Israelites. When the Israelites saw the Egyptian soldiers, they said to Moses, "Have you brought us to the wilderness to be killed?"

Moses said, "Have faith in God." He stretched his hand over the sea, and the sea split in two! The Children of Israel passed through the sea on dry ground, while the waters of the sea stood like high walls on their right and on their left.

"Follow them," Pharaoh ordered, and his soldiers drove their chariots where the Israelites had walked. But the ground turned to mud, and the wheels of the chariots stuck so that the horses could not pull them. The walls of water came crashing down on the army of Egypt, drowning the men and the horses, swallowing the chariots, and destroying the army of Egypt. And the Israelites danced and sang a song of victory to God.

❏ Motivation

Talk with your students about rules and laws. Draw the distinction between behavior that goes against our values (lying, cheating, being rude to parents) and behavior that is also punished by laws (murder, theft). Discuss how both sets of behavior can hurt others.

❏ Using the Illustration

Have the children describe in their own words what is happening to the Pharaoh's army. Do they think it is fair to let the Pharaoh's army drown? Point out that the army was attacking civilians—including women and children.

❏ Biblical Source

Exodus 13–34

❏ Background for the Teacher

The cycle of stories about Moses is the longest in the Torah. Condensing all of these chapters into three stories is difficult, but there is no doubt that this is one of the most important parts.

There is a story in the Midrash in which a search for the Torah eventually leads to Moses who claims he does not have it. When God reminds Moses that the Torah was given to him, Moses replies that he is just one man and the Torah was given to all of God's creation. This pleased God who honored Moses—the Torah is known as the Five Books of Moses.

❏ Vocabulary

chariot a two-wheeled horse-drawn vehicle used in battle in ancient times

wilderness an area in which few people live that is not suitable or not used for farming

❏ Teaching the Story

Q: Where did Moses and the Israelites camp?
They camped by the Sea of Reeds.

Q: Who chased after the Israelites?
Pharaoh and his chariots chased after the Israelites.

Q: How did the children of Israel pass through the sea?
God split the sea in two.

Q: What happened to Pharaoh's army?
The water returned and swallowed up his army.

MOSES ON THE MOUNTAIN **45**

❑ Teaching the Story

Q: Where did Moses go?
Up the mountain to receive the laws of God.

Q: What did the people do because Moses was gone so long?
They forced Aaron to make them a god made of gold.

Q: What did Moses do upon seeing the golden calf?
He shattered the tablets and burned the calf.

❑ Vocabulary

ornaments something that adorns, decorates, or adds beauty
calf a young cow
tablet a flat slab suitable for inscription
ground reduced to powder or pieces

❑ Using the Illustration

Have the children describe how Moses feels as he walks with the tablets and when he sees the people worshipping the golden calf.

❑ A Special Teaching Opportunity

How long is "three moons passed"? The calendar generally used in the modern world is a sun calendar. It measures a year by the number of days it takes for the earth to revolve around the sun (365 ¼). But since early times, Jewish months have followed the moon. It is 29 ½ days from one new moon to the next, so Jewish months are 29 or 30 days long. On each leap year, every two or three years, we add, not just a day, but an extra month (Adar II). This system keeps the moon months and the sun years in rhythm together.

Three moons passed and the people made camp at the foot of the mountain called Sinai. God said to Moses, "Come up the mountain. I will give you the laws so that you may teach them to the people."

Moses was gone a long time. The people complained to his brother Aaron. "Moses has died and left us," they said. "His God will not protect us any longer." They forced Aaron to make them a god. They brought jewelry and ornaments and Aaron formed the gold into a calf. The people made a great feast to worship their new god.

God told Moses, "Hurry down! Your people are doing evil."

Moses came down the mountain, and he was carrying two tablets of stone. The laws of God were written on the tablets. But when Moses saw the people worshipping the golden calf, he grew angry. He raised the tablets high above his head and threw them to the ground, shattering them into bits and pieces. He burned the golden calf in a fire and ground what was left into powder.

Hands-on Learning

Conducting a Seder To relate the stories of Moses to Passover, conduct a seder with your class. You'll need to plan the activity in advance as this is a good opportunity to involve parents in the teaching process by having them help in the preparation and also by having them attend the seder.

If you want an activity on a smaller scale, you can bring a seder plate to class and review the significance of each symbol. Conclude the activity by allowing the children to search for the afikomen.

46 LET'S DISCOVER THE BIBLE

God said, "Cut two tablets like the first, and I will write the laws upon them as before." So Moses made two more tablets. He rose early the next morning and climbed the mountain once again. He stayed forty days and forty nights upon the mountain, and when he returned, his face glowed with light.

Moses called Aaron and all the Children of Israel near, and he gave them the commandments that God had spoken on Mount Sinai:

I am the One God—your God—who brought you out of Egypt.
You shall have no other gods. You shall make no statue or picture to worship.
You shall not speak falsely in God's name.
Remember the Sabbath day, to keep it holy.
Honor your father and your mother.
You shall not murder.
You shall not be false to your wife or husband.
You shall not steal.
You shall not lie about your neighbors.
You shall not want the things that belong to your neighbor.

And the Children of Israel promised to be faithful to God forever. They said, "All these things we will do and we will remember."

❏ Teaching the Story

Q: What did God tell Moses after Moses shattered the tablets and ground the golden calf?
God instructed Moses to make two new tablets and climb the mountain again.

Q: What had God spoken to Moses at Mt. Sinai?
God had given Moses the commandments.

Q: What did the Children of Israel promise?
They promised they would be faithful to God forever.

❏ Vocabulary

falsely intentionally untrue, not genuine

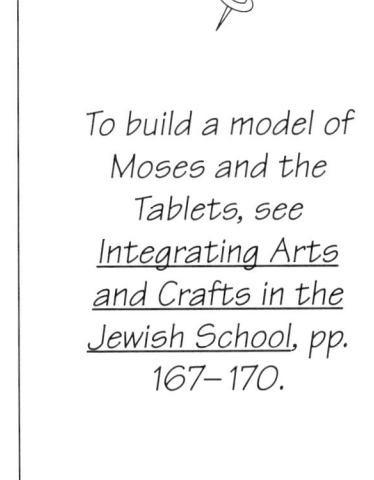

To build a model of Moses and the Tablets, see Integrating Arts and Crafts in the Jewish School, pp. 167–170.

Read More About It

"The Work of God's Hands," Exploring Our Living Past, p. 185. This story emphasizes God's love and concern for the Jewish people. But the story cautions us to be compassionate—we must not forget that all creatures, even our enemies, are "The Work of God's Hands."

"The Golden Calf," Exploring Our Living Past, p. 195. This story offers another look at the mistake made by the people of Israel while they waited for Moses to return.

"Who Will Be My Surety?" Lessons from Our Living Past, p. 11. The Jewish people made a covenant with God at Mount Sinai, and in return for the gift of the Torah, they offered their children as surety.

Activity Page

Just By Looking
The answer is Path #1. Younger children can use colored pencils or crayons to see the path more easily.

Word Find
For Readers: possible answers include NO, MAN, TEN, SAT, TEAM, COT, MOM, MET, AND, SEND
For Non-Readers: Ask the class to list as many of the Ten Commandments as they can. Complete the list for them.

C the Story
For Readers: Have a volunteer read the story aloud.
For Non-Readers: Read the story to the class.

Let's Talk About It
Discuss student responses.

A Big Question
For discussion, refer back to the motivation activity on page 45.

Let's Talk About It
Why did God give the laws a second time?
Answers will vary. God forgives the people for making the golden calf. God puts aside punishment because the people are worthy of redemption.

Just By Looking
Help the Children of Israel cross the sea.
Can you tell which path will take Moses and the Israelites across on dry land? Choose one, then trace it with your finger to see if you are correct.

Word Find
God gave us commandments.
Make 10 new words using the letters in the word **COMMANDMENTS**

C the Story Finish the story by adding the missing letter C

Moses led the __hildren of Israel out of Egypt.
The Egyptian soldiers __hased after them.
The __hildren of Israel __rossed the sea on dry ground.
But the wheels of the Egyptian __hariots got stu__k in the mud.
Later God said to Moses, "__ome up the mountain."
While Moses was gone, the people prayed to a golden __alf.
But Moses brought them God's __ommandments.
The __hildren of Israel promised to be faithful to God forever.

Let's Talk About It
The Fifth Commandment says:
HONOR YOUR FATHER AND YOUR MOTHER.
Can you think of ways you can honor your parents?

? A BIG QUESTION Why do people need rules? **?**

Family Education

Learning at Home The *Learning at Home* worksheets provide an opportunity for enriching the study of Judaism in the home. The activities found in the worksheets allow each child's family to participate in the child's education.

Distribute worksheet 11 at the end of class. Have the children bring home both the worksheet and the four-page folder containing the story of *Moses on the Mountain*.

Learning at Home worksheet available on page 87 in the back of this guide.

48 LET'S DISCOVER THE BIBLE

SAMSON

Samson took an oath, promising that he would never cut his hair. Because he kept this promise, God gave him great strength. He grew to be a mighty warrior. The Children of Israel loved Samson and called him a "Judge"—the name they used for their important leaders.

Now a people called the Philistines had troubled the Children of Israel for forty years. Samson knew this and waited for a chance to help his people. One day, a Philistine cheated him. "Now," Samson thought, "I have a reason to take revenge!" And what a revenge he took! He captured three hundred foxes and put them in pairs, tail to tail. Then he tied a torch to the tails of each pair. When the torches were blazing, he sent the foxes running through the fields of the Philistines, setting fire to all their grain.

❏ Motivation

Ask the class to list superheroes that they know. (Batman, Spiderman, Superman) Discuss what gives them their strength and for what purpose they use their superpowers. Focus the discussion on heroes that fight for good causes. Tell the class that today they will learn about a hero who had super strength from God and used his power to fight the enemy of Israel.

❏ Biblical Source

Judges 13–16

❏ Background for the Teacher

Taken out of context, the story of Samson could be considered a violent tale of an easily angered, vengeful man, certainly one who should not be given the honored title of "judge". But the Philistines were a threat to the people of Israel in the land of Canaan. The Philistines had superior strength, as can be evidenced by how easily the people of Judah give Samson to the Philistines. So Samson takes on the Philistines single-handedly so that any rage the Philistines feel at the toll exacted by Samson would be aimed at him alone, not at the people of Israel.

❏ Vocabulary

oath a solemn promise to God
revenge to get even for a wrong done
torch a portable light flaming at one end; to set ablaze

❏ Teaching the Story

Q: What oath did Samson take?
Samson swore he would never cut his hair.

Q: Because of his great strength, Samson became a mighty warrior. What did the people call him?
They called Samson "judge"—the name they used for their important leaders.

Q: How did Samson take revenge for being cheated?
He tied torches between the tails of foxes to set fire to the fields of the Philistines.

SAMSON **49**

❏ Teaching the Story

Q: What was the second action Samson took against the Philistines?
He ran through the crowd of Philistines with his sword like the foxes had run through the fields.

Q: Why did the Israelites try to give Samson to the Philistines?
The Israelites feared the Philistines.

Q: Why didn't the Philistines capture Samson?
He broke his ropes, grabbed the jawbone of a dead donkey, and slayed one thousand Philistines.

Q: With whom did Samson fall in love?
He fell in love with Delilah.

Q: What was the secret that Delilah discovered?
She discovered the secret of Samson's strength—his hair.

Samson was made a Nazirite by his parents. A Nazirite was not supposed to drink strong drinks or shave his hair. In early Jewish history, Nazirites were patriots and warriors on behalf of the Lord.

The Philistines took the man who had cheated Samson and burned him. But Samson said to them, "Again you have done evil!" And he ran through the crowd of Philistines with his sword like the foxes had run through the fields, cutting down many men.

The Philistines cried out, "Give us Samson, or we will make war on you." And the Israelites were afraid. So they tied Samson with two new ropes and put him where the Philistines could find him. But when the Philistines came near, the Spirit of God became Samson's strength. Samson raised his arms and the ropes split like old thin thread. Samson grabbed the first thing he saw—it was the jawbone of a dead donkey—and ran into the Philistine crowd, swinging the bone from side to side. When it was over, a thousand Philistines were dead.

Afterward, Samson fell in love with a woman and her name was Delilah. The Philistines said to Delilah, "Discover the secret of Samson's strength and we will pay you well."

Delilah pestered Samson day and night. "What makes you so strong?" She asked and asked. "What is your secret?" At last, Samson opened his heart and told her. "My strength comes from my hair that I have dedicated to God. My hair has never been cut."

Hands-on Learning

Have the children draw the strongest thing they know. Ask them which do they think is stronger—what they drew or Samson?

50 LET'S DISCOVER THE BIBLE

Delilah waited until Samson was asleep and then she called the Philistines to cut off his hair. When he awoke, his strength was gone.

The Philistines blinded Samson and threw him into prison. They forced him to turn a stone wheel in the mill, as if he were a donkey. But they were careless, and, day by day, Samson's hair grew longer and longer.

At last, the Philistines made a great feast in their temple. They brought Samson from the prison to laugh at him. Thousands of Philistines watched as Samson was tied between two pillars of the temple. But Samson did not laugh. He prayed, "Oh God, give me strength just one more time to take revenge for my two eyes. Let me die with the Philistines!"

Then Samson placed one hand on each of the stone pillars and pushed against them with all his might. Slowly the mighty columns moved outward. Then they broke loose and the walls came tumbling down, crushing Samson and the thousands of Philistines.

By his death, Samson killed more Philistines than he had killed in his life. And the People of Israel remembered him as one of the great Judges, for Samson had judged Israel for twenty years.

❏ Teaching the Story

Q: What did the Philistines do to Samson after they cut off his hair?
They blinded him and threw him into prison, where he turned the stone wheel in the mill as if he were a donkey.

Q: How were the Philistines careless?
They let Samson's hair grow back.

Q: What did Samson do to their temple?
He knocked the pillars down, crushing thousands of Philistines and himself.

❏ Using the Illustration

Have the children compare the scene illustrated on this page with the destruction of wicked people in the time of Noah, Sodom and Gomorrah, and the Pharaoh's army in the Sea of Reeds. What is different about this story? (The hero is also destroyed.)

Suicide is considered a sin in Judaism. Here, however, Samson's death is not considered a suicide, since it has a purpose beyond just ending his life.

SAMSON

Activity Page

Hidden Letters
For Non-Readers: Read the question aloud to get the answer DELILAH.

Which Words?
Both readers and non-readers can act out each of the words listed.

If I Were Samson
Non-readers can complete the sentences aloud.

A Big Question
Have the discussion focus on personal experiences with making and keeping promises. You may want to share one of your own.

Let's Talk About It

Was Samson doing God's work?
Answers will vary. Certainly Samson's strength comes from God—it is stated at the outset of the story—and twice he gets his strength from God. Samson used his strength to help his people, God's chosen people. In the complete text (Judges 14) it is stated that even his parents did not know that "it was at the instigation of the Lord that Samson should have occasion to quarrel with the Philistines."

HIDDEN LETTERS
Let's Discover The Bible STORY 12

Draw a straight line from **A** to **B**. Then draw another line from **C** to **D**.

Color the 7 letters **BLACK**.   Who tricked Samson?

Which Words?
Which of these words makes you think of Samson?

JUDGE	STRONG
BLIND	BRAVE
GREAT	SAD
AFRAID	ANGRY
WEAK	HAPPY

Make a sentence with each word you choose.

If I Were Samson
If I were Samson I would be very _____.
If I were Samson and I got angry, I would _____.
If I were Samson and wanted to help I would _____.
_____

? A BIG QUESTION Why is it important to keep a promise? **?**

---

52   LET'S DISCOVER THE BIBLE

Ruth and Naomi

In the days of the judges, an Israelite family went to live in the land of Moab. The father died, leaving his wife Naomi and his two sons. Each of the sons took a wife from among the women of Moab. Ten years passed, and both sons died. Naomi was left alone with her two daughters-in-law.

Naomi said to them, "Go back to your families, and I will return to my home in the Land of Israel." She hugged and kissed them and all three women began to weep. The young women said to her, "Let us go with you, to your people." But Naomi shook her head and said, "Turn back." Then one of the young women kissed Naomi and returned to her home.

❏ Motivation

Discuss the modern practice of *tzedakah* in your school and synagogue as compared to the ancient practice of gleaning in the fields by the poor.

❏ Biblical Source

Ruth 1–4

❏ Background for the Teacher

The story of Ruth and Naomi is taken from the Scroll of Ruth. The story's location within the framework of the Bible has changed over time, but the significance of the story has not been lost in the shuffle. Every year we read the Scroll of Ruth on Shavuot. There are two reasons for this tradition. First, Shavuot is a harvest festival and the main action of the story takes place during the harvest. And second, Shavuot celebrates the giving of the Torah. Ruth accepts the Law of Moses through her conversion to Judaism.

❏ Using the Illustration

Ask questions about the first part of the story using the illustration on this page. Who are the women in the picture? (Naomi and her two daughters-in-law) In what land is their tent set up? (Moab) Where will Naomi be going? (back to the Land of Israel) Where will the daughters-in-law go? (One will stay in the land of Moab; Ruth will go with Naomi.)

Point out the time setting of the story: "In the days of the judges." Remind the children that Samson was honored with the title of Judge.

❑ Teaching the Story

Q: Why did Ruth stay with Naomi?
Ruth wanted to go with Naomi to become one of her people.

Q: What season was it in Bethlehem?
It was the harvest season.

Q: What were the poor allowed to do in the fields?
They were allowed to glean which means they could pick up the grain the farm workers left behind.

Q: In whose field did Ruth glean?
Ruth gleaned in the field belonging to Boaz.

❑ Vocabulary

glean to gather what is left by the reapers, those who gather grain

---

But the other, Ruth, refused to leave. Ruth said to Naomi, "Where you go, I will go. Where you make your home, I will make my home. Your people shall be my people. And your God shall be my God. Where you die, I will die. And there I will be buried."

So together they crossed the Jordan River and came to Bethlehem. It was the harvest season. The poor went out to the fields to glean. They would pick up the grain that the farm workers left behind. Ruth told Naomi, "I will go out and glean so that we may have food." Naomi sent Ruth to the field of her relative, a rich man named Boaz.

When Boaz saw Ruth he asked his servant, "Who is this young woman?" And the servant replied, "She returned from Moab with Naomi." Then Boaz went to Ruth and said, "Glean only in my field. I have heard how you left your home in Moab to honor your mother-in-law, Naomi. God will reward you." And Boaz told his workers to leave grain behind where Ruth could find it easily.

Every day, Ruth went to the field of Boaz. And every night, she returned home with her basket filled with grain.

One night Naomi said, "Daughter, you need a home. Do as I say: Put on your best clothing and your perfume oil. Find Boaz and wait until he goes to rest. Then go to him and he will tell you what to do."

Hands-On Learning

Tzedakah The actions of Boaz were appropriate because he acted to fill a need. The mitzvah of tzedakah calls for supplying what each poor person lacks. Ruth and Naomi lacked food so Boaz, who could afford to, provided for them.

Have the children in your class decide on an act of tzedakah. Even at a young age, children can recognize that others in their community are in need. Help them select a local cause to contribute to in some small way. By selecting something within the community, it may be easier for the children to see the immediate effects of their actions.

NOW Boaz finished eating and his heart was filled with cheer. He went to rest. Ruth came up to him softly. "I am your relative, Ruth," she said. "And I need your help."

Boaz said, "Have no fear, I will help you." He went to the city gate to find Naomi's closest relative. "Either you or I must buy the land of Naomi and marry her daughter," Boaz said to the man. "It is up to you, because you are Naomi's nearest cousin. What will you do?"

"I am already married," said the man.

Boaz turned to the others in the marketplace. "You are all my witnesses," he said. "I will marry Ruth the Moabite, and give her children, to carry on our family name." And the people near the gate heard and said, "May God bless you both."

Boaz married Ruth and they had a child. Naomi loved the child as if it were her own. The people called the child Obed. And Obed was the father of Jesse. And Jesse was the father of David, who rose to become the King of Israel. This was the special blessing that God gave to Ruth who had remained loyal to Naomi and converted to the faith of the Jews.

❑ Arts and Crafts

Tell the children that this story comes from the Scroll of Ruth. Have the children make their own scrolls. Each child will need a cardboard roll and several pieces of paper. Have the children draw scenes from the story on the pieces of paper which can be taped together and onto the roll.

The children can also make models of Ruth. This activity is described on page 173 in *Integrating Arts and Crafts in the Jewish School* by Carol Tauben and Edith Abrams.

❑ Teaching the Story

Q: What did Boaz say to Naomi's closest relative?
Boaz told him that one of them had to buy Naomi's land and marry Ruth.

Q: Who married Ruth?
Boaz did.

Q: Who was their great-grandson?
David, the king of Israel, was the descendent of Ruth and Boaz.

Q: Why was Ruth given this special blessing?
Ruth remained loyal to Naomi and converted to the faith of the Jews.

❑ Vocabulary

converted   changed over to

❑ A Special Teaching Opportunity

Use the conclusion of the story to explain to the class that when people convert to Judaism, they become full-fledged Jews. Considering the vast numbers of intermarriages and conversions among our congregants, this is a subject to be treated tenderly. Both the story and the topic of conversion are important teachings for our children to begin to understand.

Read More About It

"The Story of Ruth," <u>Lessons from Our Living Past</u>, p. 31. This selection offers another version of the beautiful speech in which Ruth offers loyalty to Naomi and to the Jewish way of life.

RUTH AND NAOMI

Activity Page

Make a Sign
You can create a tzedakah display using the signs created by the children.

My Family Tree
Tie this activity into *A Special Teaching Opportunity* described on page 55. Point out that Ruth, a convert to Judaism, is the Great-Grandmother of King David, one of our greatest kings.

Food
Hidden items include grapes, an apple, a carrot, bread, and an egg cooked sunny side up.

A Big Question
Use the question to raise discussion among the children. Answers may include that tzedakah is a mitzvah; that helping others makes you feel good; or that you would want help if you were needed.

Let's Talk About It
How is a person rewarded for loyalty and devotion?
Answers will vary. Ruth was rewarded for her loyalty to Naomi and the Jewish faith—King David will be descended from Ruth.

Family Education
Learning at Home Duplicate worksheet 13 and distribute at the end of class. Have the children bring home both the worksheet and the four-page folder containing the story of *Ruth and Naomi*.

Learning at Home worksheet available on page 89 in the back of this guide.

David and Goliath

When Saul was King of Israel, people called the Philistines were Israel's greatest enemy. Once, Israel was camped on one hill, and the Philistine army was camped on another. Between them was a deep valley. In the morning, the Israelites saw a man step forward from the Philistine army— a man so huge he seemed a giant. And the man's name was Goliath.

The bronze helmet on Goliath's head shone like a jewel in the sunlight. His body was covered in gleaming armor. And when he spoke, Goliath's voice was like the roar of a rushing river.
"I am the champion of the Philistines," he cried out to the Israelites. "Choose one man to fight for Israel. Send him to fight against me!"

❏ Motivation

Have the children name stories that have a giant as a leading character. (Jack and the Beanstalk, Gulliver's Travels) Tell the children that today they will read about a boy who uses his brain and his belief in God to defeat a giant.

❏ Using the Illustration

Before reading the story, ask the children the following questions about the boy in the picture: What is his job? (He is a shepherd.) By looking at him, can you tell if he is strong? (No.) By looking at him, can you tell if he is courageous? (Probably not.) Talk about the adage that "you can't judge a book by its cover."

❏ Biblical Source

First Samuel 17–20

❏ Background for the Teacher

The story of David and Goliath is a testimony to faith in God. David triumphs over Goliath despite David's size, age, and lack of armor. David's faith in God brings him victory. As he declares, "God will help me win against the enemy of Israel." When David saw how huge Goliath was, how heavily armed, he called out "You come to me with a sword, a spear, and a javelin, but I come to you in the name of the Lord."

❏ Teaching the Story

Q: Who were Israel's greatest enemies?
The Philistines were Israel's greatest enemy.

Q: If Goliath's voice was like the "roar of a rushing river," how would you describe his size?
Answers will vary but may include "tall as a towering tree."

Q: How did Goliath challenge the Israelites?
He challenged them to send one man to fight for them.

❏ Vocabulary

camped refers to having the army temporarily stationed at that location

bronze a brownish-colored metal alloy of tin and copper; commonly used in biblical times

gleaming flashing; sudden brightness

champion a person who has defeated all opponents

❏ Teaching the Story

Q: Why wouldn't anyone in Saul's army fight Goliath?
They were afraid of the giant.

Q: Why wasn't David afraid of Goliath?
Because he had fought a lion and a bear, he thought he could defeat the giant because Goliath was "a man like any other."

Q: Who would help David defeat the giant?
David believed that God would help him.

> Have the class list words they would use to describe the Goliath. (scary, huge, tough, mean, tall, bully)

The Israelites were afraid. King Saul asked, "Who will fight Goliat But no one answered. For forty days and forty nights, Goliath came out and challenged the Israelites. And for forty days, no Israelite dared to fight against him.

At this time a young boy named David watched his father's sheep. One day David's father said, "Three of your brothers are in the army of Saul. Take some food and carry it to your brothers." Early the next morning, David did as his father asked.

As David came to the camp of the Israelites, the giant Goliath came out to challenge them once again. Goliath roared. "Who will fight against me?" And David saw that all the king's soldiers were afraid.

David asked his brothers, "Why are you frightened? This man is just a man like any other!" And King Saul heard the words that David spoke. Then Saul looked at David and said, "Your words are brave, but you are just a boy."

David said, "I have guarded my father's sheep for many years. If a lion came, or a bear, I fought against it and kept it from stealing the sheep. I have killed both lion and bear, and I will kill the Philistine giant. God will help me win against the enemy of Israel."

❏ Arts and Crafts

Sandals Point out the sandals that both David and Goliath are wearing. The children can make their own sandals using cardboard, scissors, crayons or chalk, and tape. Have each child trace each foot on the cardboard using a crayon or chalk. Cut out the tracing. Use strips of scrap paper to make the toeholds pictured in the illustration. Tell the children that this type of footwear is still commonly used in many parts of the world, except they are normally made out of leather.

Then Saul said to David, "I will let you wear my armor." So they placed Saul's helmet on David's head and Saul's armor on David's body. But it was so heavy that David could not walk.

So David took off the helmet and the armor. He took only his shepherd's stick and his slingshot, and he began walking toward Goliath. As he passed the dry river bed at the bottom of the valley, he picked up five smooth stones and put them in his bag.

As Goliath came closer, he saw that David was just a boy. He laughed and the sound of his laughter shook the hills. "Do you think I am a dog?" he called out to David. "Do you think you can kill me with a stick?"

David came closer, saying, "You come against me with a sword and a spear, but God will protect me."

As Goliath came closer still, David reached into the bag, took out a stone, put it in his slingshot, and sent it flying at Goliath. The stone sailed straight and true, striking Goliath in the center of his forehead. The giant fell to the ground. Then David took the sword that fell from Goliath's hand and used it to kill Goliath.

When the Philistines saw that Goliath was dead, they ran. And the soldiers of Israel chased after them, killing many.

And that is how God protected the army of Israel and gave them a new hero, the boy David who would soon become the next king of Israel.

Hands-on Learning

Have the children role play the story of David and Goliath. Let one child play Goliath and another play David. Other roles can be King Saul, David's father, David's brothers, Israelites, and Philistines. Remember that any role can be played by either a boy or a girl. Go through the story more than once, allowing other children to play the major roles.

❑ Teaching the Story

Q: Why didn't David wear any armor?
Saul's armor was too heavy for the boy.

Q: What weapons did David have?
David only had his shepherd's stick and his slingshot

Q: What did David do with his slingshot?
He sent a stone sailing into Goliath's forehead which knocked him down. David then killed Goliath with Goliath's sword.

❑ Vocabulary

true exactly or accurately

Read More About It

"David and the Spider," <u>Stories from Our Living Past</u>, p. 70. This story from the Midrash offers another adventure about young David before he becomes king.

"King David and the Frog," <u>Lessons from Our Living Past</u>, p. 50. King David learns from a frog that great abilities come from God.

"David and Goliath," <u>Lessons from Our Living Past</u>, p. 53. This selection offers another adaptation of the story of the young shepherd and the giant.

Activity Page

Tell the Story
For Readers: giant, David, slingshot, forehead, sword, ran, hero/king

For Non-Readers: Have the children illustrate each of the words.

A Jewish Symbol/ Connect the Dots
Talk about how the Magen David is an important symbol. Where does it appear? (the flag of Israel) What color is the star on the flag? (blue) What are other important Jewish symbols? (menorah, Torah scroll) Show the children how to draw a Magen David using two triangles. Ask if anyone in the class has a necklace or other jewelry with a Magen David. Encourage them to wear the jewelry at the next class session. (If you have one, be sure to wear it too.)

A Big Question
As the class discusses the question, encourage students to talk about the things they think are important.

Let's Talk About It
How does God reward faith?

Answers will vary. David's faith was rewarded with a victory against someone much stronger than himself. David became a hero and a king of Israel. Ask the children how they think they will be rewarded for their faith.

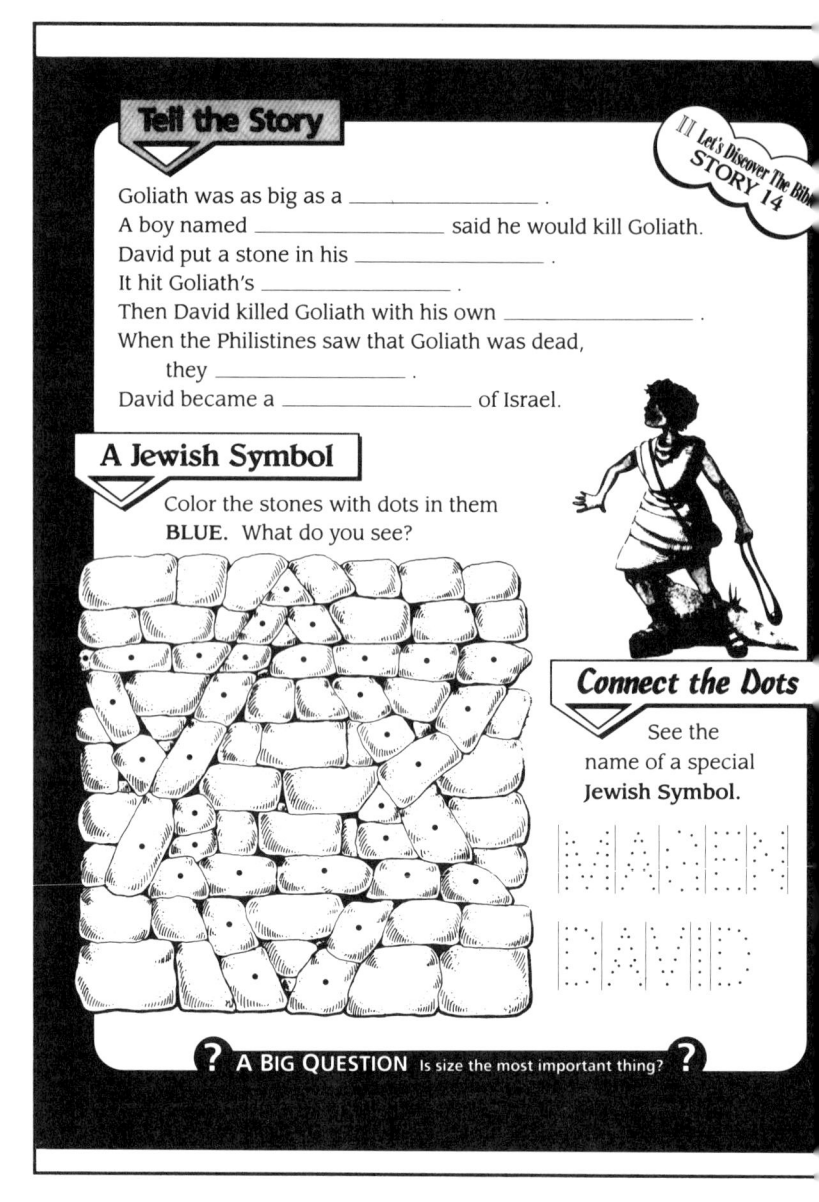

Let's Discover The Bible STORY 14

Tell the Story
Goliath was as big as a _____ .
A boy named _____ said he would kill Goliath.
David put a stone in his _____ .
It hit Goliath's _____ .
Then David killed Goliath with his own _____ .
When the Philistines saw that Goliath was dead, they _____ .
David became a _____ of Israel.

A Jewish Symbol
Color the stones with dots in them **BLUE**. What do you see?

Connect the Dots
See the name of a special **Jewish Symbol**.

M A G E N
D A V I D

? A BIG QUESTION Is size the most important thing? **?**

Family Education
Learning at Home Distribute worksheet 14 at the end of class. Have the children bring home both the worksheet and the four-page folder containing the story of *David and Goliath*.

The **Learning at Home** worksheets provide an opportunity for enriching the study of Judaism in the home. The activities found in the worksheets allow each child's family to participate in the child's education.

Learning at Home worksheet available on page 91 in the back of this guide.

60   LET'S DISCOVER THE BIBLE

Solomon, the Wise King

The first King of Israel was Saul, the farmer-king. The second was David, the warrior-king. And the third was Solomon, the son of David. In a dream one night, Solomon heard God ask, "What shall I give you?" And Solomon answered, "O God, You have already made me a king. You have already given me a great father and mother. But I know so little. So, could you give me a kind and understanding heart so that I can judge Your people with wisdom?"

And God was pleased. "Because you did not ask for gold, or long life, or death for your enemies, I will give you wisdom. And I will also give you glory and riches. You shall be the greatest of kings. And, if you walk in My ways, I will also give you long life."

❏ Motivation

Ask the children about times when they have argued with a friend or with a sibling. How did they settle the argument? Did they agree on an end to the argument together or did someone else step in to solve the problem? Was this person fair? What makes someone good at settling disputes? Encourage discussion on this topic then introduce *Solomon, the Wise King*.

❏ Biblical Source

First Kings 3–8

❏ Background for the Teacher

What is lacking in the succession of Solomon to the throne held by David is God's selection. Saul and David were anointed by Samuel, but Solomon succeeded just because he was David's son. The dream of Solomon provides for God's selection. At the end of the story, when the people thank God for giving them a wise king, God's selection is reaffirmed.

❏ Teaching the Story

Q: Who were the first three kings of Israel?
Saul, the farmer-king; David, the warrior-king; and Solomon, son of David were the first three kings of Israel.

Q: What did Solomon ask from God?
Solomon asked for a kind and understanding heart with which to judge the people.

Q: Why did God tell Solomon that he would be the greatest of kings?
Solomon did not ask for riches, long life, or the death of his enemies.

❏ Teaching the Story

Q: What was the problem that Solomon had to solve?
He had to decide who was the baby's real mother.

Q: How did he solve the problem?
By announcing that he would have the baby cut in half, Solomon got the real mother to reveal herself as the one would not want the baby harmed, even at the expense of losing the child.

Q: How did the people of Israel express their devotion to Solomon?
They loved him as long as he lived. They prayed with him, sang with him, and mourned him when he died.

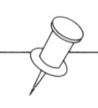

Be certain that the children understand that Solomon never intended to cut the baby in half, he was merely testing the two women.

Then Solomon awoke and knew it had been a dream. But he spoke a prayer, thanking God for the dream.

One day, when King Solomon was sitting in judgment, two women came before him to present a problem. One said, "We live together in the same house. I gave birth to a child, and three days later she also gave birth to a child. And there were only the two of us in the house. That night, her baby died. When she saw that I was asleep, she took my baby and placed her dead baby beside me. When I awoke in the morning, I saw the dead child, but he was not mine. O great and mighty king, force her to give me back my baby."

The other woman said, "No. The living baby is mine." And the two women argued back and forth.

At last Solomon said, "Bring a sword and cut the living child in two. Give one half to one woman and the other half to the other woman."

One woman said, "That's a very wise judgment, O king." But the other woman said, "No, no! Please do not hurt the baby. Give it to her, but do not cut it in half!"

King Solomon spoke again. "Now I know who is the true mother of the living child! Give the baby to the woman who refused to let it die. She is the true mother!"

Later, when the people of Israel heard the story of Solomon's judgment, they thanked God for giving them a wise king. And the people loved Solomon as long as he lived. They read the words of wisdom that he wrote. They worked to build the Holy Temple with him. They prayed with him when he prayed, sang with him when he sang, and mourned for him when he died. Even today, they still tell stories about Solomon, the wise king of Israel.

Hands-on Learning

Sitting in Judgement Have the children sit in judgement like King Solomon. Allow them to choose a problem from the Bible that can be resolved by a mock court. Examples include Esau arguing for the return of his birthright or Abraham arguing to save the good people of Sodom and Gomorrah.

Depending on the size of your class, you can have several children arguing for and several children arguing against the case. You can also have a panel of Solomons—several children sitting in judgement.

❑ Using the Illustration

Have the children use the illustration to retell the story of Solomon. If you prefer, have the children act out the scene that corresponds to the illustration.

Read More About It

"The Hoopoe's Feathers," Exploring Our Living Past, p. 203. This story shows another example of how wise Solomon was.

"King Solomon's Dinners," Stories from Our Living Past, p. 84. Even a wise man like King Solomon has lessons to learn. In this case the lesson is about hospitality.

"The Field of Brotherly Love," Lessons from Our Living Past, p. 34. When King Solomon got ready to build the great Temple, he remembered that the sages had said it would be built "in a field of brotherly love." But first he had to find that field.

SOLOMON, THE WISE KING

Activity Page

Build the Temple
Readers and non-readers alike will enjoy this activity. Allow the children to color the picture.

What Does It Mean?
Discuss how we can learn from others, especially by being good listeners.

What Is Important?
Non-readers should be able to cross off the pairs of letters. Write the remaining letters on the board and ask the question aloud, "What did Solomon ask for?" WISDOM

Compare and Find Out
Read the instructions aloud for non-readers. The differences are the headpiece; what each woman is carrying; the color of their clothing; and one is wearing sandals while the other is not.

A Big Question
Use the question to start discussion. Have the children consider what it means to be wise. Who is the wisest person in their lives, and why?

Let's Talk About It
How does the story of Solomon show respect for life? Answers will vary. The mother in the story sacrifices her claim to the child because she would prefer that the child live with the wrong mother than be harmed.

Build the Temple
Connect the dots to help King Solomon finish the Holy Temple

Let's Discover The Bible STORY 15

What Does It Mean
"Who is wise? One who learns from every person."
Avot 4:1

What Is Important?
Look at the letters in the puzzle. Cross out any letter that appears two times. Find the 6 leftover letters. They spell the answer to the question.

What did Solomon ask for?
___ ___ ___ ___ ___ ___

If God asked you, what would you choose?

Compare and Find Out
These two women look alike but are not exactly the same. How many differences can you find?

? A BIG QUESTION Why is it important to be wise? **?**

❑ Classroom Enrichment (Optional)
It is said that Solomon wrote three books of the Bible including The Book of Proverbs. Duplicate worksheet 15 and distribute to the children. First talk about the proverb in a literal sense—do they like their names? Are they *good* names? Next, talk about a good name related to a person's reputation. Then have the children make their crowns.

Enrichment worksheet available on page 93 in the back of this guide.

Jonah and the Great Fish

In the days of the prophets, a man named Jonah lived by the sea. God spoke to Jonah. "Go to the city of Nineveh," God said, "and tell them that they will be destroyed because of the evil they have done." But Jonah did not want to be a prophet. So he tried to run away from God. He got on a ship bound for a distant city and sailed away.

God sent a mighty wind and a fearful storm. The ship bobbed and tossed on the waves like a toy boat. It nearly broke in two. The sailors each prayed to his own god. The captain went to where Jonah was sleeping and yelled, "Get up and pray to your God to save us!"

❑ Motivation

When children begin to learn about God they often ask "Where is God?" In other faiths the answer is often that God is in heaven, looking down upon the people. In our Judaic faith, we teach that God is omnipresent. Pose the question, "Where is God?" to your students. Discuss their responses and use the responses to introduce the story of *Jonah and the Great Fish*.

❑ Biblical Source

Jonah 1–4

❑ Background for the Teacher

This tale of a reluctant prophet who is swallowed by a great fish is a parable. The moral lesson that the author conveys is that the God of Israel is omnipresent. At the beginning of the story, Jonah does not realize the presence of God outside of Israel, thus he tries to escape to "a distant city." Jonah learns that there is no place to hide from God—not even in the belly of a fish.

Later in the story Jonah warns Nineveh. He becomes angry when the people of Nineveh are forgiven because they heed God's warning. The lesson here and the lesson of the gourd, is that God rules all nations of the earth; God is concerned about a city of 120,000 people and about the well-being of a single plant.

❑ Vocabulary

prophet a person who speaks for God

❑ Teaching the Story

Q: Why did Jonah try to run away from God?
He did not want to be a prophet.

Q: What happened to Jonah when he tried to sail to a distant city instead of going to Nineveh?
The ship he was on was tossed by a mighty storm sent by God.

Q: When does the storm end?
The storm ends when Jonah is thrown from the ship.

❑ Teaching the Story

Q: After Jonah was thrown into the sea, a great fish swallowed him. How does he get out of the fish?
After three days, he prays to God and the fish spits Jonah out onto dry land.

Q: What does Jonah learn from this experience?
Jonah learns that there is no place to hide from God—not even in the belly of a fish.

Q: Describe the city of Nineveh.
Nineveh was so enormous that it took three days just to walk from one end to the other.

Q: What did the people of Nineveh do when Jonah warned them that their city would be destroyed?
They believed Jonah and sought God's forgiveness.

God saw that the people of Nineveh "were truly sorry" because they not only asked for forgiveness but also changed their ways.

Then Jonah confessed, "This storm is because of me, because I tried to run away from God. Throw me into the sea, and the storm will end." So they threw Jonah into the water, and the air grew still and the sea was calm.

God sent a great fish to swallow Jonah. Three days and three nights, Jonah stayed in the belly of that fish. At last, Jonah could bear no more. He prayed to God, and the fish spit him out onto dry land. "Now," God said, "go to Nineveh and deliver My message." And Jonah—who had learned that there was no place to hide from God—went to Nineveh.

What an enormous city it was. It took three days just to walk from one end to the other! Jonah entered Nineveh and walked for one full day, crying out, "In forty days, this city shall be destroyed."

The people heard Jonah and believed him. They stopped eating. They dressed in rough clothing that hurt their skin. They prayed for God to forgive them. Even the king left his throne and sat in ashes, asking for God's mercy. And when God saw the people were truly sorry for the evil they had done, God decided not to destroy the city after all.

Hands-on Learning

Provide the children with art supplies to create a bulletin board comic book display of the story of Jonah. Divide the bulletin board into squares like a page in a comic book. Assign each square to several children who have to fill in a part of the story. Scenes should include the ship in the storm and Jonah being thrown from the ship; Jonah and the great fish; Jonah warning the people of Nineveh and the people repenting; and, Jonah and the shade plant. Besides illustrating the story, include dialogue and narration as they would appear in a comic book.

In the heat of the day, Jonah climbed to the top of a hill. Then he sat down and stared at the city. He was angry. "This is just what I thought would happen," he said. "O God, You told me to say that Nineveh would be destroyed. Now You have made me a liar. You took away my honor. You should take my life, too!"

God asked, "Should you be so angry?" As Jonah sat, God made a plant grow up over him. So Jonah was grateful for the plant, because its shadow protected him from the sun. Then God sent a worm to attack the plant, and the plant shriveled and died. The next day, the sun beat down on Jonah's head again. God said, "Is it right for you to be angry about the plant?" And Jonah answered, "I am so angry that I want to die!"

But God spoke kindly. "Behold, you care about a little plant that grew up in a night and shriveled in a night. In the same way, I care about the city of Nineveh with its people that number one hundred and twenty thousand. Even though they are not wise people, even though they make mistakes, I care for them the same way that I care for you."

Read More About It

"Jonah and the Gourd," <u>Lessons from Our Living Past</u>, p. 80. This story tells what happened to Jonah after he got out of the belly of the fish.

❏ Teaching the Story

Q: **Why was Jonah angry at God?**
Because God did not destroy Nineveh, Jonah felt that his honor had been taken away.

Q: **Why was Jonah angry about the plant?**
God made the plant that provided Jonah with shade and then God took the plant away.

Q: **What lesson did Jonah learn about God because of the plant and Nineveh?**
Jonah learned that God cares equally about Nineveh and Jonah.

❏ A Special Teaching Opportunity

Jonah is not angry because God did not destroy Nineveh but because God was treating the people of Nineveh the same as Israelites were treated, despite the fact that the people of Nineveh worshipped other gods.

Take this opportunity to talk about jealousy. Ask the children if they have ever felt jealousy and anger towards a sibling because of special treatment that sibling had received from their parents. Through discussion, show that parents may give their attention to others at times but overall care equally for all of their children.

In the same way, God cares for all people because God is the God of all people, of all nations.

Activity Page

Go Fish
Help non-readers sound out the letters to decide which ones to cross out. Ask them who was swallowed by the fish? JONAH

First Letter Game
Nose, **I**ron, **N**ail, **E**lephant, **V**iolin, **E**ar, **H**ammer: NINEVEH

Jonah's Maze
Jonah has to take the middle path.

Who's Talking
1. God; **2.** the ship captain; **3.** Jonah; **4.** Jonah; **5.** God

A Big Question
Use the question to discuss behavior. How do we behave in school, on the playground, in the synagogue, and at home?

Let's Talk About It
In what way is God the God of all people? Answers will vary. God cares for all people who conduct their lives properly, as did the people of Nineveh when they repented and changed their ways. The story of Jonah teaches us to respect all people, whether they are Jewish or not.

Family Education
Learning at Home Duplicate worksheet 16 and distribute copies at the end of class. Be sure that each child brings home the worksheet and the four-page folder containing the story of *Jonah and the Great Fish*.

Learning at Home worksheet available on page 95 in the back of this guide.

LET'S DISCOVER THE BIBLE

WORKSHEETS

Family Education and Classroom Enrichment

On the following pages you will find 13 worksheets. Each is numbered to correspond to the number of the story. Select the Classroom Enrichment worksheets appropriate for your pupils and photocopy them in the quantity required for your class. You are the best judge of which ones will work in your classroom situation. The use of all of the Learning at Home worksheets is encouraged. They are a wonderful way to enrich the study of Judaism in the home.

Worksheet 1 ◆ Creation (Learning at Home) 71

Worksheet 2 ◆ Adam and Eve (Classroom Enrichment) 73

Worksheet 4 ◆ The Tower of Babel (Learning at Home) 75

Worksheet 5 ◆ Abraham and Sarah (Learning at Home) 77

Worksheet 6 ◆ Isaac and Rebecca (Classroom Enrichment) 79

Worksheet 8 ◆ Joseph and His Brothers (Classroom Enrichment) 81

Worksheet 9 ◆ Baby Moses (Hands-on Learning) 83

Worksheet 10 ◆ Let My People Go (Classroom Enrichment) 85

Worksheet 11 ◆ Moses on the Mountain (Learning at Home) 87

Worksheet 13 ◆ Ruth and Naomi (Learning at Home) 89

Worksheet 14 ◆ David and Goliath (Learning at Home) 91

Worksheet 15 ◆ Solomon, The Wise King (Classroom Enrichment) 93

Worksheet 16 ◆ Jonah and the Great Fish (Learning at Home) 95

◆ ◆ ◆ ◆ ◆

◆ Learning at Home ◆

Dear Parent,

Today your child learned about the story of Creation. We think your child will enjoy reading the story with family members at home. As you read the story folder, you will notice that the light created on the first day did not shine from the sun ("the lights in the sky" weren't created until the fourth day). The light on the first day came directly from God. When we light Shabbat candles on Friday evening, we welcome God into our homes. When you light Shabbat candles, as generations of Jews have done before, you enrich the life of your family. You may want to talk to your child about how to light Shabbat candles. The ritual blessing is printed below.

◆ Bring the Light of Creation into Your Home ◆

How to Light Shabbat Candles

Sabbath candles may be lit, at the earliest, 1¼ hours before sunset, but the usual time is up to 18 minutes before sunset.

Light the candles.

Move your hands around the flames several times and bring them toward your face. This gesture symbolically welcomes the Sabbath into your home.

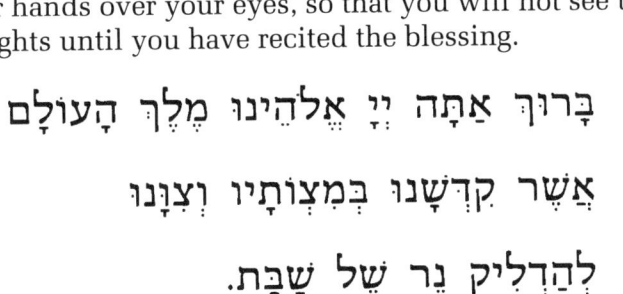

Place your hands over your eyes, so that you will not see the Sabbath lights until you have recited the blessing.

בָּרוּךְ אַתָּה יְיָ אֱלֹהֵינוּ מֶלֶךְ הָעוֹלָם

אֲשֶׁר קִדְּשָׁנוּ בְּמִצְוֹתָיו וְצִוָּנוּ

לְהַדְלִיק נֵר שֶׁל שַׁבָּת.

Baruch atah adonai elohenu melech ha-olam asher kidshanu b'mitzvotav v'tzivanu l'hadlik ner shel shabbat.

Blessed are You, Lord our God, Ruler of the Universe, Who has made us holy by giving us commandments, and has commanded us to kindle the Sabbath lights.

Worksheet 1 ◆ Creation

Name _____

For Classroom Enrichment

Fill the Trees

Trees covered with fruit grew in the Garden of Eden. Adam and Eve had delicious fruit to eat.
Fill the trees in the Garden of Eden with different kinds of fruit.

WORKSHEET 2 ◆ ADAM AND EVE

◆ Learning at Home ◆

Dear Parent,

Today your child learned about the story of the Tower of Babel. Here is another version of the story. Read it to your child and talk about it together.

The people who lived in the land of Shinar began to build a city. They took mud and shaped it into bricks, which they baked in the sun until they were dry and hard. They laid the bricks in rows and bound them together with mortar. They placed row upon row of bricks, and the walls of their buildings rose up tall and firm. This gave their king an idea. "Let us build a tower so tall that it reaches up to heaven."

"Yes, we shall build the tower!" the people shouted in reply. They worked night and day. The tower grew higher and higher. One day the king sent out a royal decree: "Let it be known that there is nothing in the world more precious than bricks!"

The royal decree made the workers very proud. "Every brick brings us closer to heaven," they said. "Indeed, bricks are better than gold."

The higher the tower grew, the greater was the value of every brick. When the tower was a mile high, it took over a year for each brick to be carried to the top. Every time a brick fell from the tower, the bricklayers wept and tore their hair. But when a worker fell from the tower, not a tear was shed.

The builders decided, "Bricks are more precious than gold, and they are more precious than people as well." This pleased the king. He sent a second decree: "Let it be known that bricks are more precious than people!"

God, who had made both people and bricks, decided to teach them a lesson. As the builders worked, their hands grew more and more slippery, and soon the bricks were falling all about. The king, who was admiring his tower from below, had to run for protection to keep from being hit by falling bricks.

The workers began to call to each other to pile the bricks up safely and stop their fall. But suddenly they could not understand each other. God had confused their tongues, and now each one spoke a different language. The workers began to argue and fight, babbling in a thousand separate languages. Their work on the tower was ended forever.

Now the king realized that God was teaching him and his people a lesson. His tower would never reach to heaven; instead, it would stand unfinished, to remind people how confused and weak they become when they work against God. It came to be called the Tower of Babel.

Then God's angels brought a decree from on high. It said, "Remember two things: truly, people are more precious than bricks and God in Heaven is greater than all the things of earth!"

Worksheet 4 ◆ The Tower of Babel

♦ Learning at Home ♦

Dear Parent,

Read the story of Abraham and Sarah with family members at home. Reread the part when Abraham says to Lot, "Let there be peace between us."

Talk with your children about the idea of keeping peace at home or *shalom bayit*. Discuss the need to share among siblings and friends and also to respect one another's feelings, privacy, and personal belongings.

Make a list with your child of things to do to keep peace in the home. Display the list in a prominent place.

Be sure to encourage and support your child when something on the list is done. You may even want to put a star or other sticker on the list to show the completion of the item.

MY SHALOM BAYIT LIST

Here are some things I will do to keep peace in our home:

_____

_____

_____

_____

_____

_____

_____

Worksheet 5 ♦ Abraham and Sarah

Name _____

For Classroom Enrichment

Color the Picture

There are 10 camels hidden in the picture. Can you find them?

WORKSHEET 6 ♦ ISAAC AND REBECCA

For Classroom Enrichment

Joseph's Brothers

Unscramble the names of Joseph's brothers.
Draw a line to the correct name.
One has been done for you.

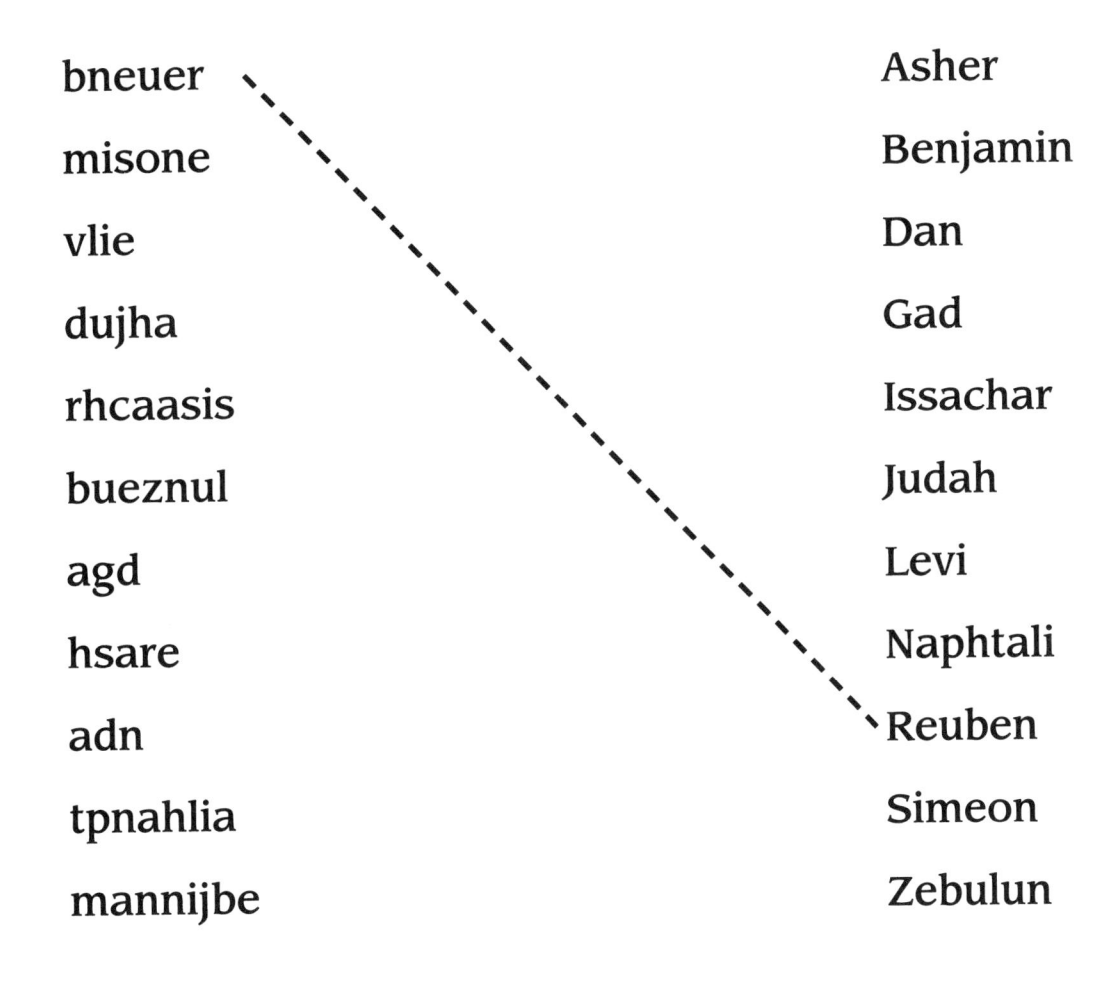

bneuer	Asher
misone	Benjamin
vlie	Dan
dujha	Gad
rhcaasis	Issachar
bueznul	Judah
agd	Levi
hsare	Naphtali
adn	Reuben
tpnahlia	Simeon
mannijbe	Zebulun

WORKSHEET 8 ◆ JOSEPH AND HIS BROTHERS

For Hands-on Learning Activity
on page 38 of this guide

Pick a Picture

WORKSHEET 9 ◆ BABY MOSES

For Classroom Enrichment

Word Find

Look across and down to find
the 10 plagues hidden in the puzzle.

```
C A T T L E A B B U
C C H D B L O O D E
L F A O G D H P A I
O F I R S T B O R N
C E L J V K L F K L
U Q M G F N I W N O
S H F P L R S Q E I
T R R A I S T J S T
S S O U E K E V S B
W L G X S T R Y M Z
I N S E C T S C A M
```

This list will help you.

BLOOD   BLISTERS
FROGS   HAIL
FLIES   LOCUSTS
INSECTS   DARKNESS
CATTLE (disease) (killing of) FIRSTBORN

WORKSHEET 10 ◆ LET MY PEOPLE GO

◆ Learning at Home ◆

Dear Parent,

Today your child has learned about the commandments that God gave to Moses on Mount Sinai. They are listed on the third page of the story folder. Take the time to read the story with your child and talk about the commandments. Afterwards, let your child color the tablets below.

You can glue this page onto a piece of cardboard. After the glue dries, you can cut out the tablets and display them.

Note that each number 1–10 has a Hebrew letter next to it. Each Hebrew letter is equivalent to the number: 1=Alef; 2=Bet; 3=Gimmel; 4=Dalet; 5=Hay; 6=Vav; 7=Zayin; 8=Chet; 9=Tet; 10=Yud.

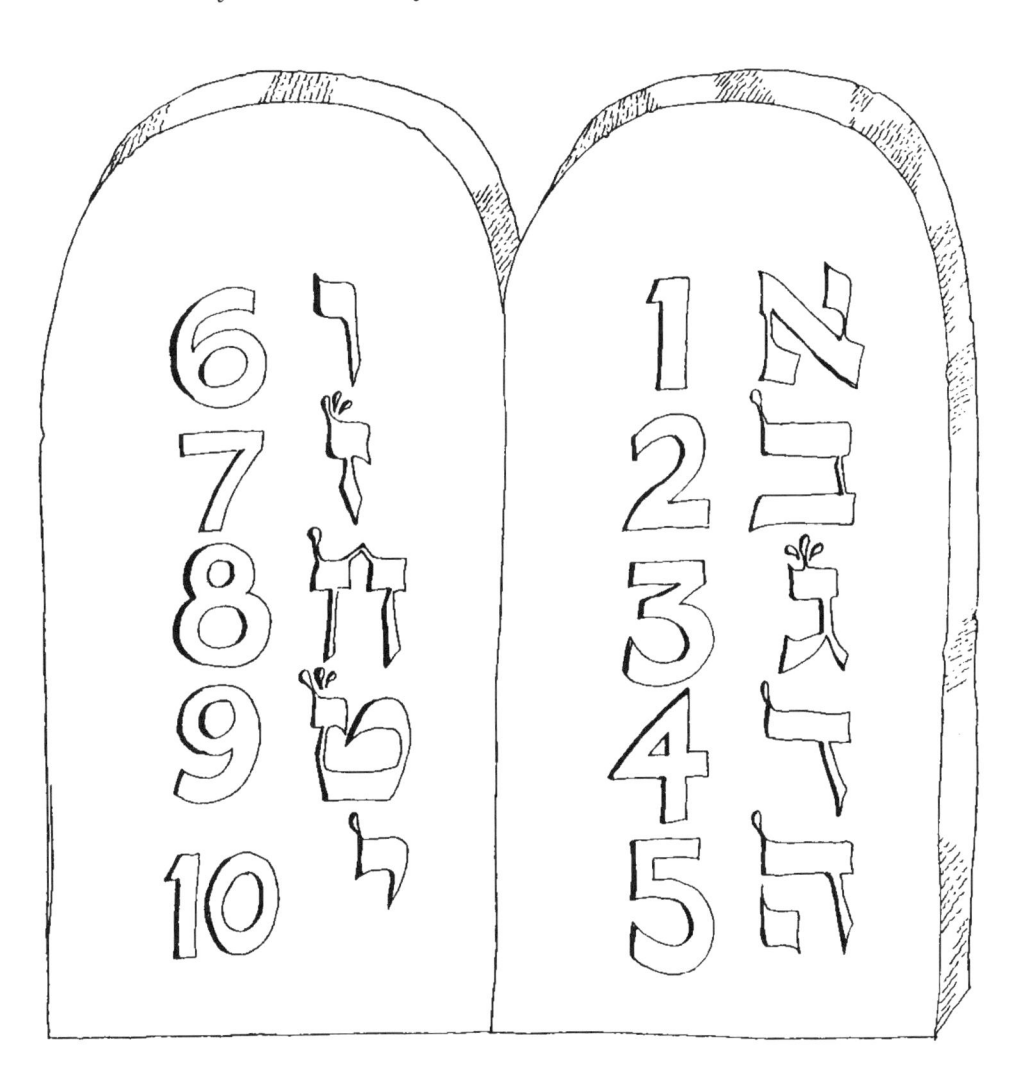

Worksheet 11 ◆ Moses on the Mountain

◆ LEARNING AT HOME ◆

Dear Parent,

Today your child learned about the Story of Ruth. You and your child will enjoy reading the story with family members at home.

The mitzvah of tzedakah calls for supplying what each poor person lacks. Ruth and Naomi lacked food, so Boaz provided for them. Boaz acted to fill their need.

We help the poor by giving tzedakah. We collect coins in a special container. When it is filled, we send the money to charity. Using the label below, help your child make a special tzedakah box. After your child has colored the picture, simply tape the label to a clean, empty juice can or container. On Friday, before the Shabbat candles are lit, encourage your child to put coins into the tzedakah box.

WORKSHEET 13 ◆ RUTH AND NAOMI

◆ LEARNING AT HOME ◆

Dear Parent,

An adventure story of a small child defeating a giant is one that will spark a child's imagination. Today your child experienced this tale through the story of David and Goliath. This adventurous tale is certain to stand out in a child's memory.

Have your child tell you the story by using the pictures in the four-page folder. Then you can read the story together.

Talk about facing challenges and why we remember those who stand up to challenges, even when there is danger involved.

You can also talk about symbols like the Magen David on the back page of the folder. You may want to take the time to make an Israeli flag out of blue and white construction paper or your child can complete and color the star and stripes blue on the one below. Then you can hang it on the refrigerator or in your child's room.

WORKSHEET 14 ◆ DAVID AND GOLIATH

Name _____

For Classroom Enrichment

A Good Name Is Better Than Just Riches
Proverbs 22:1

When we do Mitzvot, we get a SHEM TOV—a Good Name. The crown of a good name is even better than the crown of a king. Here is your crown. Color, cut out, and attach the 2 strips to the sides to make the crown. This is the crown of a SHEM TOV for you to wear.

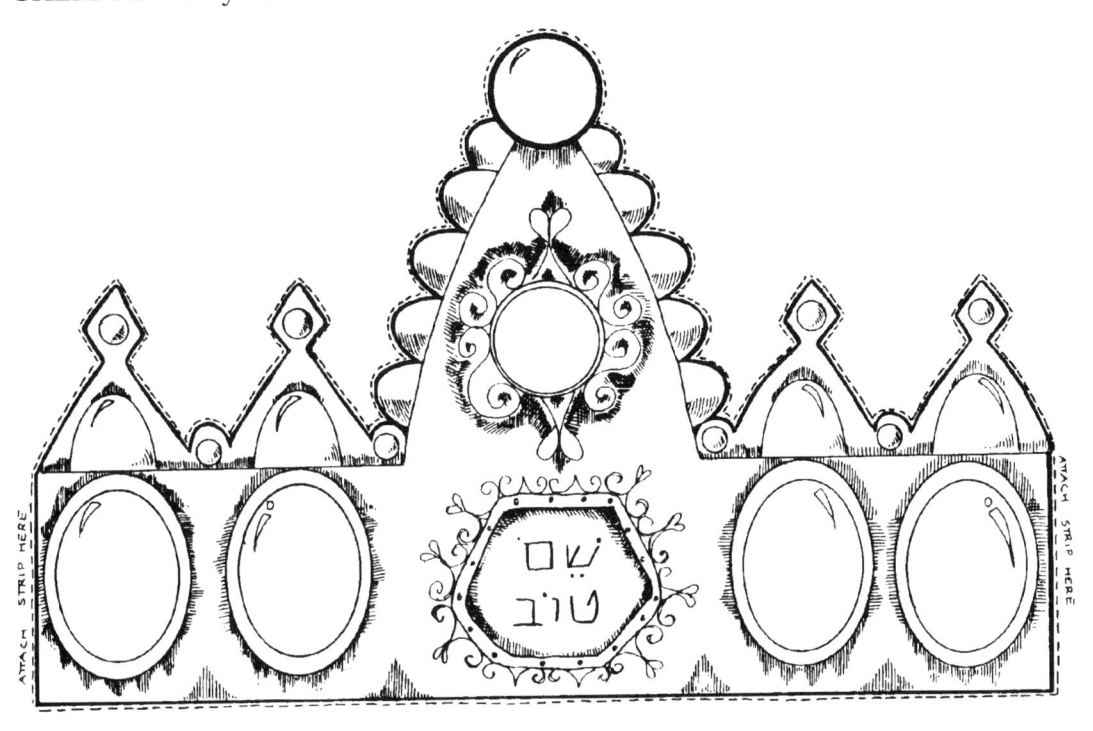

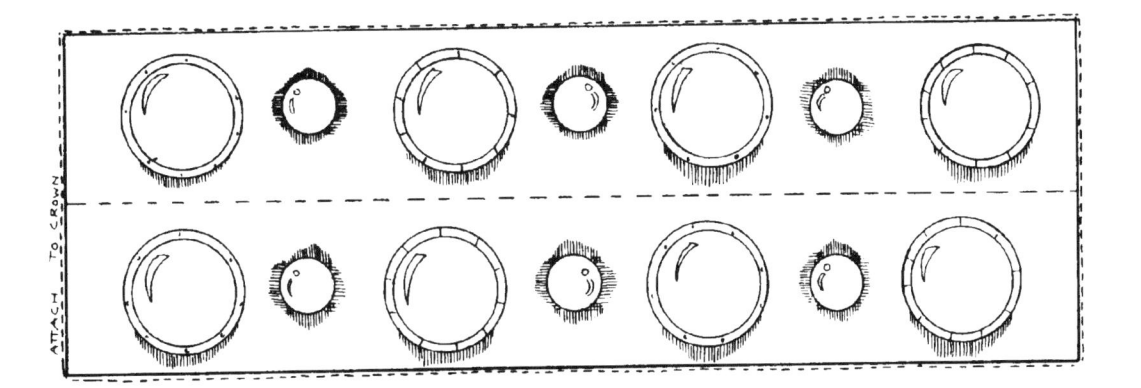

WORKSHEET 15 ◆ SOLOMON, THE WISE KING

◆ LEARNING AT HOME ◆

Dear Parent,

Today your child learned about the story of *Jonah and the Great Fish*. One of the central themes of this parable is that we should respect all people, whether they are Jewish or not. This theme is one of many that your child has learned while reading stories from the Bible.

This folder is the last of 16 Bible stories that your child has read. Take some time to review the stories by asking your child to remember details from all the stories. The story titles are listed below the questions.

What is the day of rest?

Who lived in the Garden of Eden?

Who built an ark to save the animals of the world?

How did God stop the building of the Tower of Babel?

What baby was rescued from the Nile River by Pharaoh's daughter?

What are the Ten Commandments?

How did David defeat Goliath?

What was your favorite Bible story?

Who was your favorite character from the Bible stories?

Creation ■ The Garden of Eden ■ Noah ■ The Tower of Babel
Abraham and Sarah ■ Isaac and Rebecca ■ Jacob and Esau ■ Joseph and His Brothers ■ Baby Moses ■ Let My People Go ■ Moses on the Mountain ■ Samson ■ Ruth and Naomi ■ David and Goliath
Solomon, the Wise King ■ Jonah and the Great Fish

WORKSHEET 16 ◆ JONAH AND THE GREAT FISH